Acting Edition

NOËL COWARD'S
THE RAT TRAP

REIMAGINED BY
BILL ROSENFIELD

Copyright © 2026 by Bill Rosenfield
Cover design © 2026 by Rebecca Pitt
All Rights Reserved

THE RAT TRAP is fully protected under the copyright laws of the British Commonwealth, including Canada, the United States of America, and all other countries of the Copyright Union. All rights, including professional and amateur stage productions, recitation, lecturing, public reading, motion picture, radio broadcasting, television, online/digital production, and the rights of translation into foreign languages are strictly reserved.

ISBN 978-0-573-00097-3

concordtheatricals.co.uk
concordtheatricals.com

FOR AMATEUR PRODUCTION ENQUIRIES
United Kingdom and World
excluding North America
licensing@concordtheatricals.co.uk
020-7054-7298

Each title is subject to availability from Concord Theatricals Corp., depending upon country of performance. Please be aware that *THE RAT TRAP* may not be licensed by Concord Theatricals Corp. in your territory. Professional and amateur producers should contact the nearest Concord Theatricals Corp. office or licensing partner to verify availability.

CAUTION: Professional and amateur producers are hereby warned that *THE RAT TRAP* is subject to a licensing fee. The purchase, renting, lending or use of this book does not constitute a license to perform this title(s), which license must be obtained from the appropriate agent prior to any performance. Performance of this title(s) without a license is a violation of copyright law and may subject the producer and/or presenter of such performances to penalties. Both amateurs and professionals considering a production are strongly advised to apply to the appropriate agent before starting rehearsals, advertising, or booking a theatre. A licensing fee must be paid whether the title is presented for charity or gain and whether or not admission is charged.

This work is published by Samuel French, an imprint of Concord Theatricals Ltd.

The Professional Rights in this play are controlled by Alan Brodie Representation, 14 Red Lion St, London WC1R 4QH
www.alanbrodie.com | ABReception@alanbrodie.com

The original version of *The Rat Trap* is available from ABReception@alanbrodie.com

No one shall make any changes in this title for the purpose of production. No part of this book may be reproduced, stored in a retrieval system, scanned, uploaded, or transmitted in any form, by any means, now known or yet to be invented, including mechanical, electronic, digital, photocopying, recording, videotaping, or otherwise, without the prior written permission of the publisher. No one shall share this title, or part of this title, to any social media or file hosting websites.

The moral right of Noël Coward and Bill Rosenfield to be identified as author of this work has been asserted in accordance with Section 77 of the Copyright, Designs and Patents Act 1988.

USE OF COPYRIGHTED MUSIC

A licence issued by Concord Theatricals to perform this play does not include permission to use the incidental music specified in this publication. In the United Kingdom: Where the place of performance is already licensed by the PERFORMING RIGHT SOCIETY (PRS) a return of the music used must be made to them. If the place of performance is not so licensed then application should be made to PRS for Music (www.prsformusic.com). A separate and additional licence from PHONOGRAPHIC PERFORMANCE LTD (www. ppluk.com) may be needed whenever commercial recordings are used. Outside the United Kingdom: Please contact the appropriate music licensing authority in your territory for the rights to any incidental music.

USE OF COPYRIGHTED THIRD-PARTY MATERIALS

Licensees are solely responsible for obtaining formal written permission from copyright owners to use copyrighted third-party materials (e.g., artworks, logos) in the performance of this play and are strongly cautioned to do so. If no such permission is obtained by the licensee, then the licensee must use only original materials that the licensee owns and controls. Licensees are solely responsible and liable for clearances of all third-party copyrighted materials, and shall indemnify the copyright owners of the play(s) and their licensing agent, Concord Theatricals Ltd., against any costs, expenses, losses and liabilities arising from the use of such copyrighted third-party materials by licensees.

IMPORTANT BILLING AND CREDIT REQUIREMENTS

If you have obtained performance rights to this title, please refer to your licensing agreement for important billing and credit requirements.

NOTE

This edition reflects a rehearsal draft of the script and may differ from the final production.

TROUPE

Troupe was founded in 2013 by Ashley Cook and presents new plays and stage adaptations, alongside rediscovered work by classic writers. Troupe's latest work at Park Theatre includes *The Forsyte Saga Parts 1 and 2* by Shaun McKenna and Lin Coghlan, based on the books by John Galsworthy, which transferred to the Royal Shakespeare Company Swan Theatre, Stratford-upon-Avon, and a commission of a new adaptation of Christopher Isherwood's *A Single Man* by Simon Reade. Other recent work includes *The Sweet Science of Bruising* by Joy Wilkinson at Southwark Playhouse, which transferred to Wilton's Music Hall and *Rasheeda Speaking* by Joel Drake Johnson at Trafalgar Studios, which starred Tanya Moodie, Elizabeth Berrington, Sheila Reid and Bo Poraj. Other productions at Southwark Playhouse include the centenary year revival of *Dear Brutus* by J. M. Barrie and *The Cardinal* by James Shirley, directed by Justin Audibert, which starred Stephen Boxer and Natalie Simpson for which she won the Ian Charleson Award. It was supported by an inaugural MGCfutures Bursary Award. Troupe's previous rediscoveries at the Finborough Theatre include Rodney Ackland's *After October*, Robert Bolt's *Flowering Cherry* and R. C. Sherriff's *The White Carnation*, which later transferred to Jermyn Street Theatre. Troupe has been nominated for a total of fourteen Off West End Awards.

★★★★★ 'Sumptuous, panoramic, intense, amusing… a masterpiece' Dominic Maxwell – *The Times* on *The Forsyte Saga Parts 1 and 2*

★★★★★ 'A gorgeous, beautifully acted epic' Dominic Cavendish – *The Telegraph* on *The Forsyte Saga Parts 1 and 2*

★★★★★ 'The most enthralling, intense five hours I have spent in a theatre this year' Georgina Brown – *Daily Mail* on *The Forsyte Saga Parts 1 and 2*

★★★★★ 'Dramatic storytelling of the highest order' Neil Norman – *Daily Express* on *The Forsyte Saga Parts 1 and 2*

★★★★★ 'One of the best new plays I have seen in years… Wonderful' Neil Norman – *Daily Express* on *The Sweet Science of Bruising*

★★★★ 'Isherwood's tale impresses on stage… a strong ensemble… glorious' Clive Davis – *The Times* on *A Single Man* (Critics' Pick of the Week)

★★★★ 'Highly recommended… fiercely intelligent' Alun Hood – *WhatsOnStage* on *Rasheeda Speaking*

★★★★ 'A riveting piece of theatre' Claire Allfree – *The Telegraph* on *The Cardinal* (Critics' Choice)

TroupeTheatreCompany
troupetheatrecompany
@Troupe_Theatre

To hear about our shows visit our website and subscribe to our mailing list www.troupetheatre.co.uk

Troupe receives no public subsidy. If you would like to donate towards or invest in one of our shows there are a number of packages for supporters.

For more information please email Ashley Cook:
ashley.cook@troupetheatre.co.uk

***The Rat Trap* at Park Theatre was made possible by the generosity of these supporters:**

Super Troupers
Ros and Alan Haigh
Sir Derek Jacobi
Boris Karloff Charitable Foundation
Dame Joanna Lumley
John R Murray Charitable Trust
Old Possum's Practical Trust
Robert and Olivia Temple

Troupers
Broughton Family Charitable Trust
Sir Jonathan Cohen

Angel Troupers
Charlotte Aitken Trust
Jane Applegarth
Stephen and Elizabeth Cook
Joan Major
Sarig Peker
Stage One
Stage Presence Ltd.
Trish Wadley

STAGE ONE

The producers of *The Rat Trap* wish to acknowledge financial support from Stage One, a registered charity that invests in new commercial productions. Stage One supports new UK theatre producers and productions, and is committed to securing the future of commercial theatre through educational and investment schemes. Stage One would like to thank all producers, theatre owners and productions that voluntarily contribute to the levy which support this investment. For further information please visit www.stageone.uk.com

Stage One is the operating name of the Theatre Investment Fund Ltd, a registered charity no. 271349

PARK THEATRE

★★★★★ **'A five-star neighbourhood theatre'** – *Independent*

Park Theatre was founded by Artistic Director, Jez Bond and Creative Director Emeritus, Melli Marie. The building opened in May 2013 and, with 10 West End transfers (including *Rose* starring Maureen Lipman, *The Boys in the Band* starring Mark Gatiss and *Pressure* starring David Haig), two National Theatre transfers, an RSC transfer and 14 national tours in its first 12 years, has garnered a reputation as a key player in the London theatre scene. Park Theatre has been awarded numerous Offie Awards, West End Wilma's Accessible Theatre Award, The Stage's Fringe Theatre of the Year and Campaign of the Year Awards, as well as receiving seven Olivier Award nominations.

We are a welcoming and accessible venue, delivering work of exceptional calibre in the heart of Finsbury Park. We work with brilliant writers, directors and artists to present compelling, exciting and beautifully told stories in our two intimate spaces. Our programme focuses on new writing, revivals of modern classics alongside a commitment to presenting joyful, entertaining shows for audiences from all walks of life. We produce our own shows, as well as working in partnership with emerging and established theatre producers. We contribute to the broader theatre industry by offering mentoring, support and opportunities to artists.

Our Creative Engagement programmes seek to widen the number and range of people who participate in creative activities, and provide opportunities for those with little or no prior contact with the arts. In everything we do we aim to be warm and inclusive; a safe, welcoming and wonderful space to work, create and visit. Park Theatre has been accredited by the Mayor of London as a Dementia Friendly building.

As a registered charity (number 1137223) with no regular public subsidy, we rely on the kind support of our donors and volunteers. To find out how you can get involved visit parktheatre.co.uk, or scan this QR code.

Staff

Artistic Director . . . . Jez Bond
Executive Director . . . . Catherine McKinney
Producer & Programmer . . . . Joshua Goodman
Programming & Producing Coordinator . . . . Ellen Harris
Development Manager (Individuals) . . . . Alannah Lewis
Creative Engagement Manager . . . . Carys Rose Thomas
Finance Director . . . . Elaine Lavelle
Finance Officer . . . . Nicola Brown
Finance Assistant . . . . Pinar Kurdik
General Manager . . . . Tom Bailey
Deputy General Manager . . . . David Hunter
Administrator . . . . Mariah Sayer
Duty Venue Managers . . . . Amber De Ruyt, David Hunter, Shaun Joynson, Wayne Morris, Zara Naeem and Laura Riseborough
Park Pizza Supervisors . . . . Toby Schuster and Alistair Bourne
Park Pizza Team Members . . . . Ewan Brand, Tessa Doubleday, Bradly Doko, George Gehm, Jordon Goodlitt, Owen McCabe, Benjamin McCann, Ruairi McGonagle, Anika McIntosh, Maddie Stoneman, Saron Tariku and Harry Taylor
Sales & Marketing Director . . . . Dawn James
Sales & Marketing Director (Maternity Cover) . . . . Nicci Allt
Head of Ticketing . . . . Matthew Barker
Sales & Ticketing Manager . . . . Lou Egan
Marketing Manager . . . . Monique Walker
Marketing Officer . . . . Eliza Jones
Box Office Supervisors . . . . Belinda Clark, Jacquie Cassidy, Natasha Green, Gareth Hackney, Trelawny Kean and Maddie Stoneman
Public Relations . . . . Mobius Industries
Technical & Buildings Manager . . . . Gianluca Zona
Deputy Technical & Buildings Manager . . . . Teddy Nash
Venue Technician . . . . Michael Bird

Trustees

Anthony Clare (Chair)
Jonathan Edwards (Vice Chair)
Ibukun Alamutu
Professor Kurt Barling
Hedda Beeby
Kathleen Heycock
Jacqueline Hurt
Joe Smith
Julia Tyrrell
Pia Richards-Glöckner

Founding President .... Jeremy Bond (1939–2020)

With thanks to all of our supporters, donors and volunteers.

CAST

DANIEL ABBOTT | Edmund Crowe

Daniel trained at LAMDA.

Theatre credits include: *Fanny* (King's Head Theatre); *Linck & Mülhahn* (Hampstead Theatre); *Are You As Nervous As I Am?* (Greenwich Theatre); *Groan Ups* (National Tour); *The Tempest* and *Measure for Measure* (Guildford Shakespeare Company); *The Lion in Winter* (English Theatre Frankfurt); *Wasted* (Orange Tree Theatre, Richmond); *Pride and Prejudice* (Open Air Theatre, Regent's Park); *Richard II*, *Henry IV Part I*, *Henry IV Part II*, *Henry V* and *The Famous Victories of Henry V* (Royal Shakespeare Company); *The Green Children* and *Progress* (The Avenue Theatre, Ipswich) and *Wuthering Heights* and *The Comedy of Errors* (Red Rose Chain).

Television credits include: *Silo*, *Erased: WW2's Heroes of Colour*, *Marcella*, *Save Me* and *Holby City*.

GINA BRAMHILL | Olive Lloyd-Kennedy

Gina trained at RADA.

Theatre credits include: *Much Ado About Nothing* (Royal Shakespeare Company); *Who's Afraid of Virginia Woolf* (Theatre Royal Bath); *Edmond de Bergerac* (Birmingham Rep and National Tour); *Bad Jews* (Theatre Royal Bath, St James Theatre and Arts Theatre); *'Tis Pity She's a Whore* (Cheek by Jowl); *Chicken* (Southwark Playhouse) and *Six Characters in Search of an Author* (Headlong).

Film credits include: *Shoshana*, *Northern Comfort*, *Pleasure Island*, *The Wedding Video*, *Red Lights*, *Lotus Eaters* and *Made in Dagenham*.

Television credits include: *Beyond Paradise*, *Bait*, *Miss Fallaci*, *The Flatshare*, *Avenue 5*, *Silent Witness*, *Us*, *Agatha and the Midnight Murders*, *Kate & Koji*, *Black Mirror*, *Sherlock*, *Brief Encounters*, *The Living and the Dead*, *Father Brown*, *The Increasingly Poor Decisions of Todd Margaret*, *Endeavour*, *Mr Selfridge*, *Being Human*, *Without You*, *Pete Versus Life* and *Victoria Wood's Midlife Christmas*.

ZOE GORIELY | Ruby Raymond

Zoe trained at École internationale de théâtre Jacques Lecoq and Royal Welsh College of Music and Drama.

Theatre credits include: *As Long As We Are Breathing* (Arcola Theatre) and *Catalyst* (The North Wall Arts Centre, Oxford).

Television credits include: *Trigger Point*.

AILSA JOY | Naomi Frith-Bassington

Ailsa trained at RADA.

Theatre credits include: *Noises Off* (National Tour); *As You Like It*, *Boatman Town* and *Antigone* (Creation Theatre); *Top Girls* (Liverpool Everyman); *Love and Other Acts of Violence* (Donmar Warehouse); *Bad Jews* (Theatre Royal Bath, National Tour and Theatre Royal Haymarket); *Jack and the Beanstalk* (The Theatre, Chipping Norton); *The Three Musketeers* and *A Midsummer Night's Dream* (Iris Theatre); *Not Quite Jerusalem* (Finborough Theatre); *The Two Gentlemen of Verona* and *A Midsummer Night's Dream* (Guildford Shakespeare Company); *TimePlays* (Hampton Court Palace); *Berenice* (The Space); *The Wind in the Willows* (Polka Theatre); *Fast Track*, *'Tis Pity She's a Whore* and *Peer Gynt* (The North Wall Arts Centre, Oxford); *Much Ado About Nothing*, *Arabian Nights* and *Pride and Prejudice* (The Drill Hall) and *The Sirens' Call* (Watermill Theatre, Newbury).

Television credits include: *Plebs* and *The Royals*.

EWAN MILLER | Keld Maxwell

Ewan trained at Royal Conservatoire of Scotland.

Theatre credits include: *Octopolis* (Hampstead Theatre); *Much Ado About Nothing* (National Theatre); *The Comedy of Errors*, *A Christmas Carol* and *Joke* (Citizens Theatre, Glasgow) and *Milkshake* (Traverse Theatre, Edinburgh).

Film credits include: *One Shot* and *Close*.

Television credits include: *Crime*, *The Gray House* and *Debriefing the President*.

LILY NICHOL | Sheila Brandreth

Lily trained at ArtsEd.

Theatre credits include: *The Other Boleyn Girl* (Chichester Festival Theatre); *Henry VI Part I*, *Maydays*, *Imperium 1: Conspirator* and *Imperium 2: Dictator* (Royal Shakespeare Company); *Blood Wedding* (Salisbury Playhouse); *If We Were Older* (National Theatre) and *Julius Caesar* (Crucible Theatre, Sheffield).

Television credits include: *3 Body Problem*, *Code of Silence*, *Death in Paradise*, *Renegade Nell*, *Maternal*, *Lockwood & Co*, *The South Westerlies* and *I Hate Suzie*.

ANGELA SIMS | Burrage

Angela trained at Guildhall School of Music and Drama.

Theatre credits include: *Gaslight, Improbable Fiction, Stepping Out, A Party to Murder, Absent Friends, Building Blocks, Season's Greetings* and *Ten Times Table* (The Mill at Sonning); *A Star Danced* and *The Wizard of Oz* (Watermill Theatre, Newbury); *Blithe Spirit* (Octagon Theatre, Bolton); *Jack and the Beanstalk* (The Roses Theatre, Tewkesbury); *Henceforward, Communicating Doors* and *And a Nightingale Sang* (Swan Theatre, Worcester) and *The Wizard of Oz* (Castle Theatre, Wellingborough).

Film credits include: *Cruella, The Little Stranger, Dreams of a Life* and *Stoned*.

Television credits include: *Dreamland, Vera, Back, Call the Midwife, Living the Dream, The Crown, Chickens, Frankie, Psychoville, Law & Order: UK, Casualty, New Tricks, Margaret Thatcher: The Long Walk to Finchley, The Bill, EastEnders, Murder in Mind, The Queen's Nose, Happiness, Cry Wolf, Great Expectations, London's Burning, McCallum* and *Five Children and It*.

Radio credits include: *Mrs McGinty's Dead, Gaudy Night, The Adventure of the Christmas Pudding, Three Act Tragedy, Stage Fright, Dead Man's Music* and *A Murder is Announced*.

CREATIVE & PRODUCTION

NOËL COWARD | Playwright

Noël Peirce Coward was born in 1899 and made his professional stage debut as Prince Mussel in *The Goldfish* at the age of 11, leading to many child actor appearances over the next few years. During that time he began to write plays, often in collaboration with his friend Esmé Wynne. His first West End play, *I'll Leave It to You* (1920), had a short run at the New (now Noël Coward) Theatre. Other plays written around that time included *The Rat Trap* which was written in 1918 but not produced until 1926.

Coward's breakthrough as a playwright came with the controversial *The Vortex* (1924) which featured themes of drugs and adultery and made his name as both actor and playwright in the West End and on Broadway. During the 1920s and 1930s, Coward wrote a string of successful plays, musicals and intimate revues including *Fallen Angels* (1925), *Hay Fever* (1925), *Easy Virtue* (1925), *This Year of Grace* (1928) and *Bitter Sweet* (1929). His professional partnership with childhood friend, Gertrude Lawrence, started with the musical revue *London Calling!* (1923) and was followed by *Private Lives* (1930) and *Tonight at 8.30* (1935).

During World War II, he remained a successful playwright, screenwriter and director, as well as entertaining the troops and even acting as a spy for the Foreign Office. His plays during these years included *Blithe Spirit* (1941), which ran for 1997 performances, outlasting the War (a West End record until *The Mousetrap* overtook it), *This Happy Breed* and *Present Laughter* (both 1942). His two wartime screenplays, *In Which We Serve*, which he co-directed with the young David Lean as well as starring in, and *Brief Encounter* quickly became classics of British cinema.

However, the post-war years were more difficult. Austerity Britain – the London critics determined – was out of tune with the brittle Coward wit. In response, Coward reinvented himself as a cabaret and TV star, particularly in America, and in 1955 he played a sell-out season in Las Vegas featuring many of his most famous songs, including *Mad About the Boy*, *I'll See You Again* and *Mad Dogs and Englishmen*. This was followed by three live television specials on CBS including *Together With Music* with Mary Martin. In the mid-1950s he settled in Jamaica and Switzerland and enjoyed a renaissance in the early 1960s becoming the first living playwright to be performed by the National Theatre, when he directed *Hay Fever* there. Late in his career he was lauded for his roles in a number of films including *Our Man in Havana* (1959) and his role as the iconic Mr Bridger alongside Michael Caine in *The Italian Job* (1969).

Writer, actor, director, film producer, painter, songwriter, cabaret artist as well as an author of verse, essays, autobiographies and a novel, he was called by close friends 'The Master'. His final West End appearance was *Suite in Three Keys* in 1966, which he wrote and starred in. He was knighted in 1970 and died peacefully in 1973 in his beloved Jamaica.

For further information on Noël Coward's life and work, visit www.noelcoward.com

BILL ROSENFIELD | Reimaginer

Bill returns to Park Theatre after his play *Another America* (published by TRW) premiered here in 2022. Other plays include *46 Beacon* (Hope Theatre and Trafalgar Studios, published by Samuel French); *Sunshine and Shadow* and *True Fans* (Blank Theatre, Los Angeles); *Let Me* (Asolo Theatre, Sarasota) and the inexplicably popular one-act *Bridal Terrorism* (published by Samuel French).

He has written two concert adaptations for the New York City Center *Encores!* series, the first was for Frank Loesser's musical *The Most Happy Fella* and the second is this year's presentation of the musical *High Spirits* based upon Noël Coward's *Blithe Spirit*.

From 1990 to 2009, he was responsible for over 65 Original Cast Recordings (25 of which received Grammy nominations) including *Assassins*, *Chicago* (revival), *Cabaret* (revival), *Ragtime*, *The Last Five Years*, *Parade*, *The Full Monty*, *Titanic*, *The Who's Tommy*, *Thoroughly Modern Millie*, *The Color Purple*, *Legally Blonde*, *Passing Strange*, *Curtains*, *Songs for a New World*, *The 25th Annual Putnam County Spelling Bee*, *Marie Christine*, *Caroline, or Change*, *Hair* (revival) and most recently Stephen Sondheim's final musical *Here We Are*.

He is featured alongside his late husband Gary Gunas in the popular series *Old Show Queens* (@oldshowqueens) and recently he was Theatrical Research Advisor on Josh Safdie's film *Marty Supreme* (A24). He is the recipient of two Drama Desk Awards, a Richard Rodgers Award and an SDC Foundation Governor's Award. He lives in North London with his husband Kishore Walker.

KIRSTY PATRICK WARD | Director

Productions for Troupe include: *The Sweet Science of Bruising* (Wilton's Music Hall and Southwark Playhouse).

Theatre credits include: *Manic Street Creature* which won a Scotsman Fringe First Award, a Stage Edinburgh Award and a Mental Health Fringe Award (Kiln Theatre, Southwark Playhouse and Summerhall Edinburgh); *The Gang of Three* (King's Head Theatre); *The Children* and *Moonlight and Magnolias* (Nottingham Playhouse); *Strike!* (Southwark Playhouse); *Groan Ups* (Vaudeville Theatre, National Tour and Centrál Színház, Budapest); *One Man, Two Guvnors* (Royal Welsh College of Music and Drama); *Spiderfly* (Theatre503); *The Comedy About a Bank*

Robbery (National Tour); *Table* (Liverpool Institute for Performing Arts); *Exactly Like You* which won the VAULT Festival Spirit Award (Underbelly Edinburgh and The Vaults); *Chef* which won a Scotsman Fringe First Award (Underbelly Edinburgh and Soho Theatre); *I'm Not That Kind of Guy* (The Vaults and Paines Plough); *Mary Louise* (The Vaults); *Evita* (MT4Uth, Belfast); *Comets* which won the IdeasTap Summer Brief (Latitude Festival); *People Like Us* (Pleasance London); *Snow White* (National Tour for The Old Vic); *A Writer's Response to 'Chavs' by Owen Jones* (Lyric Theatre, Hammersmith and Latitude Festival); *Present Tense* (Live Theatre); *Life Support* (York Theatre Royal) and *Old Vic New Voices: The 24 Hour Plays* (The Old Vic). Theatre credits as Associate Director include: *The Comedy About a Bank Robbery* (Criterion Theatre); *Present Laughter* (Theatre Royal Bath and National Tour); *Brideshead Revisited* (English Touring Theatre and York Theatre Royal); *Communicating Doors* (Menier Chocolate Factory); *Theatre Uncut: Flagship Tour* (Soho Theatre and National Tour); *Symphony* (Watch This Space at National Theatre and Latitude Festival) and *Young Pretender* (Underbelly Edinburgh and National Tour). Theatre credits as Assistant Director include: *Arcadia* (English Touring Theatre); *Othello* and *King Lear* (Shakespeare's Globe); *Our New Girl* (Bush Theatre); *Bunny* which won a Scotsman Fringe First Award (nabokov, Underbelly Edinburgh and National Tour) and *The Boy on the Swing* (Arcola Theatre). Theatre credits as Dramaturg include: *Shebeen* which won the Alfred Fagon Award (Nottingham Playhouse and Theatre Royal Stratford East). Kirsty is a graduate of the National Theatre Studio Directors Course, took part in National Theatre Connections, was shortlisted for the J. P. Morgan Award for Emerging Directors and was a finalist for the JMK Award. She also took part in the Old Vic New Voices T. S. Eliot US/UK Exchange.

LIBBY WATSON | Set and Costume Designer

Libby trained at Wimbledon School of Art and Bristol Old Vic Theatre School. Theatre credits include: *...Earnest?*, *The History Boys* and *Three Sisters* (National Tours); *The Gang of Three* (King's Head Theatre); *Tony! [The Tony Blair Rock Opera]* (Park Theatre, Leicester Square Theatre and National Tour); *Strike!* (Southwark Playhouse); *The Fellowship* (Hampstead Theatre); *KVAKK!?!* (Rogaland Teater, Stavanger); *Bring It On: The Musical* (Queen Elizabeth Hall); *Nigel Slater's Toast* (The Other Palace and National Tour); *Being Mr Wickham* (Jermyn Street Theatre, National Tour and 59E59 Theaters, New York City); *Doctor Faustus* (Sam Wanamaker Playhouse); *Trolle* and *Helt Privat* (Kilden Teater, Kristiansand); *The Philanthropist* and *The Mountaintop* which won an Olivier Award for Best New Play (Trafalgar Studios); *A Midsummer Night's Dream*, *One Man, Two Guvnors*, *Sweet Charity*, *It's a Wonderful Life* and *Guys and Dolls* (New Wolsey Theatre, Ipswich); *Once* (New

Wolsey Theatre, Ipswich, Queens Theatre, Hornchurch and National Tour); *Daisy Pulls It Off* (Park Theatre); *Peter Pan* (Misi Producciones, Bogotá); *Fences* (Theatre Royal Bath, Duchess Theatre and National Tour); *The Sisterhood, Marriage, Stars in the Morning Sky* and *The Miser* (Belgrade Theatre, Coventry); *Rudy's Rare Records* (Birmingham Rep and Hackney Empire); *Propaganda Swing* (Belgrade Theatre, Coventry and Nottingham Playhouse); *Frankie & Johnny in the Clair de Lune* (Chichester Festival Theatre); *Play Mas* (Orange Tree Theatre, Richmond); *Feed the Beast* and *Hysteria* (Birmingham Rep); *Gem of the Ocean, Blues for Mr Charlie, Radio Golf, Es & Flo* and *The War Next Door* (Kiln Theatre); *One Monkey Don't Stop No Show* (Kiln Theatre, Crucible Theatre, Sheffield and National Tour); *Blonde Bombshells of 1943* (Hampstead Theatre and National Tour) and *Blest Be the Tie* and *What's in the Cat* (Royal Court Theatre). Film and television credits include: *Alexander Pope: Rediscovering a Genius* and *Tell Me You Love Me*.

JAMIE PLATT | Lighting Designer

Jamie trained at Royal Welsh College of Music and Drama. Theatre credits include: *The Last Five Years* (Southwark Playhouse, Garrick Theatre and International Tour); *Jellyfish* (National Theatre); *Midnight in the Garden of Good and Evil* (Goodman Theatre, Chicago); *RIDE* (Southwark Playhouse, Charing Cross Theatre and The Old Globe, San Diego); *Something Rotten! in Concert* and *Pippin in Concert* (Theatre Royal Drury Lane); *Word-Play* (Royal Court Theatre); *Who's Afraid of Virginia Woolf?* (Curve Theatre, Leicester); *The Hunchback of Notre Dame in Concert* (Prince Edward Theatre); *Something Rotten!, Suddenly Last Summer* and *Sister Act* (English Theatre Frankfurt); *The Children* and *Moonlight and Magnolias* (Nottingham Playhouse); *Footballers' Wives: The Musical* (The Assembly Rooms Edinburgh); *Pride and Prejudice* and *Kes* (Octagon Theatre, Bolton and National Tour); *The White Chip, Our House, Manic Street Creature, Strike!, Beast* and *Klippies* (Southwark Playhouse); *The Harmony Test, Octopolis, Nineteen Gardens, Either, Paradise* and *Yous Two* (Hampstead Theatre); *The Rape of Lucretia, The Elixir of Love, Blond Eckbert* and *The Snowmaiden* (Hackney Empire and National Tour); *The Barber of Seville* (Nevill Holt Opera); *Kinky Boots* (New Wolsey Theatre, Ipswich); *The Gang of Three* (King's Head Theatre); *That Face* (Orange Tree Theatre, Richmond); *Cowboys and Lesbians, SUS, Never Not Once, Gently Down the Stream* and *Alkaline* (Park Theatre); *Sleeping Beauty* and *Mythic* for which he was nominated for a Knight of Illumination Award and a BroadwayWorld Award for Best Lighting Design (Charing Cross Theatre); *The Gap, Head Over Heels* and *Vincent River* (Hope Mill Theatre, Manchester); *Fame* (Birmingham Hippodrome); *Anna Karenina* (Guildhall School of Music and Drama); *My Fair Lady* and *Singin' in the Rain* (The Mill at Sonning); *One Who Wants to Cross, Checkpoint Chana, Quaint Honour, P'yongyang,*

We Know Where You Live and *Chicken Dust* (Finborough Theatre); *Daniel's Husband* (Marylebone Theatre) and *Ragdoll* and *Something in the Air* (Jermyn Street Theatre). Theatre credits as Associate Lighting Designer include: *Frozen: The Musical* (Theatre Royal Drury Lane and International Tour); *Six* (Arts Theatre and International Tour); *Born With Teeth* and *The Starry Messenger* (Wyndham's Theatre); *Ink* (Duke of York's Theatre); *The Night of the Iguana* (Noël Coward Theatre) and *Bitter Wheat* (Garrick Theatre). Jamie has been nominated for five Off West End Awards for Best Lighting Design.

ED LEWIS | Sound Designer and Composer

Ed studied at the University of Oxford and trained as a composer and sound designer at Bournemouth Media School. Theatre credits include: *The Box of Delights* (Wilton's Music Hall and Royal Shakespeare Company); *Inside No. 9 Stage/Fright* (Wyndham's Theatre and National Tour); *A View from the Bridge* (Theatre Royal Bath and Theatre Royal Haymarket); *Killer Joe* and *A Day in the Death of Joe Egg* (Trafalgar Studios); *The Best Man* (Playhouse Theatre); *The Resistible Rise of Arturo Ui* and *Force Majeure* (Donmar Warehouse); *Only an Octave Apart, A Christmas Carol* and *The Child in the Snow* (Wilton's Music Hall); *Notes from a Small Island, Othello* and *Visitors* (Watermill Theatre, Newbury); *Broken Glass* (Palace Theatre, Watford); *Darker Shores, Amongst Friends, Platinum, Ignorance/Jahiliyyah, On the Rocks* and *Alligators* (Hampstead Theatre); *King Hamlin* and *Almost, Maine* (Park Theatre); *Table* (New Vic Theatre, Newcastle-under-Lyme); *Scarlett* (Hampstead Theatre and Clwyd Theatr Cymru); *Fool for Love, Bug, Unfaithful* and *The Dazzle* (Found111); *The Vertical Hour* and *Remarkable Invisible* (Theatre by the Lake, Keswick); *The Rubenstein Kiss* (Nottingham Playhouse); *Baddies: The Musical, Breaking the Ice, Hannah, My Mother Medea, Minotaur, The Caucasian Chalk Circle* and *My Father, Odysseus* (Unicorn Theatre); *Chef* which won a Scotsman Fringe First Award (Underbelly Edinburgh and Soho Theatre); *Abigail's Party* (Curve Theatre, Leicester); *The Speed Twins* (Riverside Studios); *Gravity* (Birmingham Rep); *A Midsummer Night's Dream* (Southwark Playhouse); *Measure for Measure* (Sherman Theatre, Cardiff); *Once Upon a Time in Wigan* and *Sixty Five Miles* (Paines Plough at Hull Truck) and *Krapp's Last Tape* and *Spoonface Steinberg* (Hull Truck).

INGRID MACKINNON | Movement Director

Theatre credits as Movement Director and Choreographer include: *Private View* and *Typical* (Soho Theatre); *Twelfth Night, Princess Essex* for which she won a Black British Theatre Award for Best Movement Director, and *The Duchess of Malfi* (Shakespeare's Globe); *Noughts & Crosses, Every Leaf A Hallelujah* and *Romeo and Juliet* for which she won a Black British Theatre Award for Best Choreographer (Open Air Theatre,

Regent's Park); *Apex Predator* (Hampstead Theatre); *Toto Kerblammo!* (Unicorn Theatre); *Skeleton Crew* and *Trouble in Butetown* (Donmar Warehouse); *The School for Scandal, The Merry Wives of Windsor, First Encounters: The Merchant Of Venice* and *Kingdom Come* (Royal Shakespeare Company); *Underdog: The Other Other Brontë* (National Theatre); *The Big Life* and *Red Riding Hood* (Theatre Royal Stratford East); *Dreaming and Drowning* (Bush Theatre); *Choir Boy* (Bristol Old Vic); *Portia Coughlan* and *Reimagining Cacophony* (Almeida Theatre); *Shooting Hedda Gabler* (Rose Theatre, Kingston); *That Face* (Orange Tree Theatre, Richmond); *The Meaning of Zong* (The Barbican Theatre, Bristol Old Vic and National Tour); *Blue* (English National Opera); *Further than the Furthest Thing* (The Young Vic); *Enough of Him* (National Theatre of Scotland); *A Dead Body in Taos* (Fuel Theatre); *The Darkest Part of the Night* and *Girl on an Altar* (Kiln Theatre); *Playboy of the West Indies* (Birmingham Rep); *Moreno* (Theatre503); *Antigone* (Mercury Theatre, Colchester); *Liminal* (King's Head Theatre); *Liar Heretic Thief* (Lyric Theatre, Hammersmith); *Josephine* (Theatre Royal Bath); *#WeAreArrested* (Arcola Theatre and Royal Shakespeare Company) and *The Border* (Theatre Centre). Theatre credits as Intimacy Director include: *Eureka Day* (Nottingham Playhouse); *Private View* and *Super High Resolution* (Soho Theatre); *Les Vêpres Siciliennes, Faust* and *Festen* (Royal Opera House, Covent Garden); *The Importance of Being Earnest* (National Theatre and Noël Coward Theatre); *Twelfth Night, Princess Essex* and *The Duchess of Malfi* (Shakespeare's Globe); *Evita* (London Palladium); *Here We Are, Coriolanus, The House of Bernarda Alba* and *Phaedra* (National Theatre); *Shucked, Noughts & Crosses, Brigadoon, La Cage aux Folles, Robin Hood, The Tempest, Every Leaf A Hallelujah, Once on This Island, Antigone, 101 Dalmatians, Legally Blonde* and *Carousel* (Open Air Theatre, Regent's Park); *The Great Gatsby* (London Coliseum); *Apex Predator* (Hampstead Theatre); *The Tempest* and *Much Ado About Nothing* (Theatre Royal Drury Lane); *Natasha, Pierre and the Great Comet of 1812* and *Skeleton Crew* (Donmar Warehouse); *Wolves on Road* (Bush Theatre); *The Real Thing* (The Old Vic); *Romeo and Juliet* (Duke of York's Theatre); *Choir Boy* (Bristol Old Vic); *Shooting Hedda Gabler* (Rose Theatre, Kingston); *Sunset Boulevard* (Savoy Theatre); *That Face* (Orange Tree Theatre, Richmond); *The Effect* (National Theatre and The Shed, New York City); *Tina – The Tina Turner Musical* (Aldwych Theatre and National Tour); *Es & Flo* (Wales Millennium Centre, Cardiff and Kiln Theatre); *Enough of Him* (National Theatre of Scotland) and *Girl on An Altar* (Kiln Theatre). Ingrid holds an MA in Movement: Directing and Teaching from Royal Central School of Speech and Drama.

CLAIRE LLEWELLYN | Fight Director

Theatre credits include: *The Harder They Come* (Theatre Royal Stratford East); *Cinderella, Peter Pan, Beauty and the Beast* and *The Caucasian Chalk Circle* (Rose Theatre, Kingston); *Romeo and Juliet* and *The*

Lieutenant of Inishmore (Liverpool Everyman); *Rough Magic* and *Midsummer Mechanicals* (Shakespeare's Globe); *The Code, Unfortunate* and *The Walworth Farce* (Southwark Playhouse); *The Queen of Spades* (Garsington Opera); *The Fair Maid of the West* (Royal Shakespeare Company); *The Unseen* (Riverside Studios); *Red Speedo* and *Duet for One* (Orange Tree Theatre, Richmond); *Oliver!* and *Never Have I Ever* (Chichester Festival Theatre); *Art* (National Tour); *Wonder Boy* (Bristol Old Vic and National Tour); *Macbeth* (Leeds Playhouse); *Feral Monster* (Welsh National Theatre); *Hir, Jack and the Beanstalk* and *Whodunnit [Unrehearsed]* (Park Theatre); *Pride and Prejudice* (*sort of)* (Criterion Theatre and International Tour); *Maud* and *Down in the Valley* (Scottish Youth Opera); *Peter Pan* (Reading Rep Theatre); *Around the World in 80 Days* (Theatre by the Lake, Keswick and Hull Truck); *Kidnapped* (National Theatre of Scotland); *Oklahoma!* (Wyndham's Theatre); *71 Coltman Street* (Hull Truck); *Carmen* (Opera North) and *Don Giovanni* (Nevill Holt Opera). Theatre credits as Associate Fight Director include: *Witness for the Prosecution* (London County Hall); *2:22 A Ghost Story* (Gielgud Theatre, National Tour and Ireland Tour); *Life of Pi* (National Tour) and *To Kill a Mockingbird* (Gielgud Theatre, Leeds Playhouse and National Tour).

CAROLINE HANNAM | Costume Supervisor

Caroline trained at The Arts Institute at Bournemouth. Theatre credits as Costume Supervisor include: *Charlie and the Chocolate Factory* (Grimaldi Forum, Monte-Carlo); *The Sound of Music* (Curve Theatre, Leicester); *The Talented Mr Ripley, …Earnest?, Magic Goes Wrong, Hairspray, Once, The Cat and the Canary, Dreamboats and Petticoats, Driving Miss Daisy, The Rise and Fall of Little Voice, The History Boys* and *Footloose* (National Tours); *The Mousetrap* (St Martin's Theatre and National Tour); *Wilko: Love and Death and Rock 'n' Roll* (Southwark Playhouse and Leicester Square Theatre); *The Great British Bake Off Musical* (Everyman Theatre, Cheltenham and Noël Coward Theatre); *Tony! [The Tony Blair Rock Opera]* (Park Theatre, Leicester Square Theatre and National Tour); *Strike!* (Southwark Playhouse); *West Side Story* (Ljubljana Festival); *Evita* (International Tour); *The Last Tango* (Phoenix Theatre and National Tour); *Sweet Charity* (New Wolsey Theatre, Ipswich); *Dance 'Til Dawn* (Aldwych Theatre and National Tour) and *Midnight Tango* (Aldwych Theatre, Phoenix Theatre and National Tour). Theatre credits as Head of Wardrobe include: *Charlie and the Chocolate Factory* (Grimaldi Forum, Monte-Carlo); *Dear England* (The Lowry, Salford); *The Lehman Trilogy* (Gillian Lynne Theatre and International Tour); *The Pirates of Penzance, The Midnight Bell, Rough Crossing, Cabaret* and *Acorn Antiques: The Musical!* (National Tours); *The Confessions* (European Tour); *The Great British Bake Off Musical* (Everyman Theatre, Cheltenham and Noël Coward Theatre); *Saving Grace* (Riverside Studios); *Chicago* (Ljubljana

Festival); *Saturday Night Fever* (Peacock Theatre); *The Exorcist* (Phoenix Theatre and National Tour); *Hairspray* (Shaftesbury Theatre) and *Driving Miss Daisy* (Wyndham's Theatre).

LOIS SIME | Stage Manager

Lois trained at Guildhall School of Music and Drama. Theatre credits include: *My First Ballet: Swan Lake* (English National Ballet); *Lovestuck* (Theatre Royal Stratford East); *Mother Goose* (Hackney Empire); *Old Bridge*, *Invisible* and *Statues* (Bush Theatre); *Clybourne Park* (Park Theatre); *The Last Word* (Marylebone Theatre); *Ready, Steady, Go!* (Polka Theatre and European Tour); *The Game of Love and Chance* (Arcola Theatre); *The Prince* (Southwark Playhouse); *For Tonight* (Adelphi Theatre); *Mr Stink* (Chickenshed Theatre); *The Mosinee Project* (New Diorama Theatre); *Magical Merlin* (Fortune Theatre) and *Benidorm Live!* and *You Bury Me* (National Tours).

JULIA WILKENS | Assistant Stage Manager

Julia trained at Royal Central School of Speech and Drama. Theatre credits include: *Peter Pan* (Castle Theatre, Wellingborough); *Beauty and the Beast* (BEAM Theatre, Hertford) and *Pygmalion* (The Stag Theatre, Sevenoaks).

MOLLY NICE | Assistant Stage Manager

Molly is training at Mountview Academy of Theatre Arts. Theatre credits include: *The Paddington Bear Experience* (London County Hall); *So You've Found Me* (Lion and Unicorn Theatre); *Dick Whittington* (Bocking Village Hall) and *Sunday in the Park with George*, *A Midsummer Night's Dream* and *Next to Normal* (Mountview Academy of Theatre Arts).

ABIGAIL GRIMES | Assistant Stage Manager

Abigail is training at Mountview Academy of Theatre Arts. Theatre credits include: *The Welkin* (Mountview Academy of Theatre Arts); *Clueless The Musical* (Trafalgar Theatre); *Why Am I So Single?* (Garrick Theatre) and *Kathy and Stella Solve a Murder* (Ambassadors Theatre).

NATASHA WERBLOW | Assistant Stage Manager

Natasha is training at Mountview Academy of Theatre Arts. Theatre credits include: *Carrie* and *Faustus: That Damned Woman* (Mountview Academy of Theatre Arts); *Rodney Black: Who Cares? It's Working* (Arcola Theatre and The Bristol Improv Theatre); *Carousel* (Birmingham City Academy); *10 Stories High* (TheSpace @ Niddry Street Edinburgh); *Outlying Islands* (Jermyn Street Theatre); *Our House* (Southwark Playhouse); *Spring Awakening* (Tobacco Factory Theatre, Bristol);

Carrie (The Loco Klub, Bristol); *Frolickes of Narnia* (Winston Theatre, Bristol) and *Iphigenia* (Wickham Theatre, Bristol). Television credits include: *Double the Money*.

KYLE SMITH | Assistant Director

Kyle is training at East 15 Acting School. Theatre performance credits include: *Cabaret* (Sierra Repertory Theatre); *Much Ado About Nothing* (Vermont Shakespeare Company); *Forever Plaid* (Pacific Conservatory Theatre); *Next to Normal* (Midtown Arts Center, Eugene) and *Life Could Be a Dream* (Oregon Cabaret Theatre, Ashland).

LEWIS CHAMPNEY | Production Manager

Productions for Troupe include: *The Forsyte Saga Parts 1 and 2* and *A Single Man* (Park Theatre).

Lewis trained at Royal Central School of Speech and Drama. Theatre credits include: *Farewell Mister Haffmann*, *23.5 Hours* and *Sorry We Didn't Die at Sea* (Park Theatre); *Gods of Salford* (The Lowry, Salford); *Cutting the Tightrope* (Arcola Theatre and Edinburgh International Festival); *As Long As We Are Breathing* and *Gigi & Dar* (Arcola Theatre); *Puppy* (King's Head Theatre); *The Three Musketeers* (Oxford Playhouse); *Captain Amazing* (Southwark Playhouse); *Sweeney Todd: The Demon Barber of Fleet Street*, *A Very Expensive Poison* and *Next to Normal* (Mountview Academy of Theatre Arts) and *Lysistrata* (Royal Central School of Speech and Drama). Opera credits include: *The Little Zombie Girl* (Shaw Theatre) and *Eugene Onegin* (Jacksons Lane Arts Centre). Theatre credits as as Assistant and Associate Production Manager include: *When It Happens to You*, *The Marilyn Conspiracy*, *Whodunnit [Unrehearsed] 3* and *Kim's Convenience* (Park Theatre); *The Quest* (Shaw Theatre); *Rinaldo* and *Pandora's Box* (Royal Academy of Music); *The Odyssiad* and *The Hobbit* (Oxford Playhouse); *Some Demon* (Arcola Theatre); *Here* (Southwark Playhouse); *Dick Whittington* and *Killing Jack* (Queen's Theatre, Hornchurch) and *A Playlist for the Revolution*, *Sleepova* and *Paradise Now!* (Bush Theatre).

The World Premiere production of this reimagined version of Noël Coward's *The Rat Trap* opened on Wednesday, 28 January 2026 at Park Theatre and was produced by Ashley Cook for Troupe Productions Ltd. The cast was as follows:

OLIVE LLOYD-KENNEDY . . . . Gina Bramhill
SHEILA BRANDRETH . . . . Lily Nichol
KELD MAXWELL . . . . Ewan Miller
NAOMI FRITH-BASSINGTON . . . . Ailsa Joy
EDMUND CROWE . . . . Daniel Abbott
BURRAGE . . . . Angela Sims
RUBY RAYMOND . . . . Zoe Goriely

Creative and Production Team

Reimaginer . . . . Bill Rosenfield
Director . . . . Kirsty Patrick Ward
Set and Costume Designer . . . . Libby Watson
Lighting Designer . . . . Jamie Platt
Sound Designer and Composer . . . . Ed Lewis
Movement Director . . . . Ingrid Mackinnon
Fight Director . . . . Claire Llewellyn
Costume Supervisor . . . . Caroline Hannam
Stage Manager . . . . Lois Sime
Assistant Stage Manager . . . . Julia Wilkens
Assistant Stage Manager . . . . Molly Nice
Assistant Stage Manager . . . . Abigail Grimes
Assistant Stage Manager . . . . Natasha Werblow
Assistant Director . . . . Kyle Smith
Production Manager . . . . Lewis Champney
Producer . . . . Ashley Cook

Production Acknowledgements

Marketing | Richard Fitzmaurice and Anne Dillow for Mobius Industries
Press and PR | Kate Morley and Katie McDonagh for Kate Morley PR
Production Image Photography | Michael Wharley Photography
Production Image and Programme Graphic Design | Rebecca Pitt Creative
Publicity, Rehearsal and Production Photography | Mitzi de Margary
Production Insurance | Robert Israel for Gordon & Company
Production Accountancy | Lois Hargreaves for Collins & Company
Bookkeeping | Magita Constantine and Michelle Brooks for Collins & Company

The first production of *The Rat Trap* opened at the Everyman Theatre, Hampstead on Monday, 18 October 1926. The play was presented by Raymond Massey, Allan Wade and George Carr, who also directed, with the following cast:

SHEILA BRANDRETH . . . . .Joyce Kennedy
KELD MAXWELL . . . . .Robert Harris
OLIVE LLOYD-KENNEDY . . . . Mary Robson
BURRAGE . . . . Clare Greet
NAOMI FRITH-BASSINGTON . . . . .Elizabeth Pollock
EDMUND CROWE. . . . . Raymond Massey
RUBY RAYMOND. . . . . Adrianne Allen

THANKS TO

Alan Brodie, Alison Lee and Ella Radley at Alan Brodie Representation, Jez Bond, Amelia Cherry, Joshua Goodman, Dawn James, Nicci Allt, Monique Walker, Eliza Jones, Tom Bailey, David Hunter, Gianluca Zona and Matthew Barker at Park Theatre, Kim Poster, Robert and Olivia Temple, Oliver Soden, Blueprint Pictures, National Theatre Studio, Rita Patrocinio, Tom Hendryk, Evelien Van Camp, Becca Lymbourides, Emma Leon, Andrew Berekdar, Sir John Soane's Museum, Kishore Walker, Stephen and Elizabeth Cook, Oliver Cook and Keiron Cooke.

A WORD FROM THE REIMAGINER

Noël Coward was 18 years old when he wrote *The Rat Trap* in 1918. Eight years later, after his great success with *Hay Fever*, *The Vortex* and *Fallen Angels* it was produced to a decidedly mixed reception for a two week run at the Everyman Theatre in Hampstead. However, he didn't see it as he was in New York.

The Rat Trap was first published in 1924 as part of the Contemporary British Dramatist series (Vo. 13). That initial publication was dedicated to a promising young actress, Meggie Albanesi, a close friend of Coward's who, rumour has it, died from complications of a botched abortion. Her close friend, Lorn Lorraine, became Coward's personal secretary for the next 40 years.

In 2006 it was finally produced in London at the 50 seat Finborough Theatre where it, as before, received a mixed critical reception. I happened to see it and to be honest I found it to be over-written and dull. And yet in 2021, in conjunction with the lavish Coward Exhibition at Guildhall Art Gallery, I couldn't resist the temptation to attend a 'Rehearsed Reading' of the play. It was still over-written, but thanks in good part to a youthful diverse cast in contemporary dress, it was far from dull. I found that it leaned more toward 'Ibsen' than what we now think of as 'Coward'.

I wrote to Alan Brodie (who alongside Alison Lee manages the Coward Estate) and told them my thoughts about the play. They, in turn, offered me the opportunity to explore the play and see what I could do with it. I dove in and soon realised that this was an important rediscovery in the Coward canon. Written at the end of the Edwardian era the play addresses the very modern idea of women having an equal place alongside men in society. It highlights themes of the subjugation of women with a frankness which is, unfortunately, still relevant to today's audiences.

From this very early effort Coward was depicting human relationships (be they romantic, platonic, or artistic) with a characteristic confidence, incisiveness, and wit, which would later be more maturely addressed in plays such as *Private Lives*, *Hay Fever*, *Design for Living* and *Present Laughter*.

My 'reimagining' of the play allowed me to cut or revise a significant amount of dialogue which had detracted from the deeper themes within the work. Something that in retrospect Coward might have done at some later date. In the first volume of his autobiography *Present Indicative* Coward stated:

'It is not without merit. There is some excruciatingly sophisticated dialogue in the first act of which, at the time, I was inordinately proud. From the point of view of construction, it is not very good except for the two principal quarrel scenes. The last act is an inconclusive shambles.'

I hope that I've satisfactorily rectified those flaws and in the process have given a new life to one of our great playwright's earliest works.

– Bill Rosenfield, 2026

CHARACTERS

SHEILA BRANDRETH
KELD MAXWELL
OLIVE LLOYD-KENNEDY
BURRAGE
NAOMI FRITH-BASSINGTON
EDMUND CROWE
RUBY RAYMOND

SETTING

ACT ONE – Olive Lloyd-Kennedy's flat in Kensington
ACT TWO – The study of the Maxwells' house in Belgravia, six months later.
ACT THREE – The same as Act Two, one year later
ACT FOUR – The living room of 'Iverna Cottage', The Lizard, Cornwall, four months later.

TIME

The early 1920s.

REIMAGINER'S NOTES

All roles can be played by actors of any ethnicity, but Sheila should be played by an actor from the Global Majority.

The Reimaginer would like to dedicate this work to Alan Brodie and Alison Lee who gave him the opportunity and honour to collaborate with 'The Master'.

ACT ONE

(The drawing-room of **MRS OLIVE LLOYD-KENNEDY**'s *flat in West Kensington.)*

*(***OLIVE**, **SHEILA** *and* **KELD** *are just finishing dinner.)*

OLIVE. Now, I'll give you a toast. I only want to wish you both absolute unclouded happiness – I feel a little sad when I think of Sheila leaving me, we've been awfully happy together. But Keld dear, I trust you to look after her always, she's worth it.

SHEILA. Thank you, Olive darling. Keld?

KELD. I'll only just say thank you – like Sheila.

SHEILA. I'm glad my last night of blessed singleness has been like this, just with the two people I love best in the world. All today has been deliciously free from fuss. I always imagined a wedding eve to be full of boxes with their lids off, and new frocks lying over the backs of chairs and bright girlish bridesmaids asking foolish questions.

OLIVE. It would be like that if you were having an ordinary orthodox performance in church. Weddings are the most horribly indelicate affairs; why on earth can't people marry privately and give a reception to their well-wishers when they return from their honeymoon?

KELD. I know what you mean; it's unpleasant to feel that when the couple have arrived at their destination the relatives and friends all sit at home and say "I wonder if they'll go out tonight." A honeymoon is a thing for two, and no one else should know anything at all about it.

SHEILA. *(Raptly.)* Oh, Keld, just think of it – our Cornwall. I'm so thankful we both love it; it would have been awful if you had wanted Devon.

OLIVE. But South Devon is very sweet darling. It has nice red cliffs and a blue postcardy sea with little boats, and it's all very sunny and pretty.

SHEILA. I wonder if Cornwall will ever get civilized and horrible.

KELD. I suppose so, some day, now that the labour classes are so firmly getting the upper hand; all the beauty of England is bound to be spoilt eventually.

OLIVE. *(Rising.)* Well, let's leave these depressing remains now; isn't it comforting to feel that we have done the right thing, oozed sentiment over one another and drunk toasts. It gives one such a lovely glow of satisfaction to feel thoroughly in the picture, even over a trifle.

SHEILA. Do you consider our marriage a trifle?

OLIVE. Marriage nowadays is nothing but a temporary refuge for those who are uncomfortable at home. Come in here so that the servants can clear away.

SHEILA. I thought it was her evening out?

OLIVE. No dear, every *second* Tuesday, you ought to know by this time. By the way, Naomi Frith-Bassington wants to come up for a while this evening.

KELD. Who is she?

OLIVE. A placid creature who writes fiercely sensuous novels; she's bringing her man with her.

SHEILA. What kind of man – husband, father, brother, or only lover?

OLIVE. Only lover. They live in mild unassuming sin on the first floor. They'd much rather be married really, but someone once told them that free love was Bohemian. His name is Edmund Crowe. He writes poems for very inferior art periodicals and haunts the Poetry Bookshop.

KELD. That brands him as a *minor* literary at once.

SHEILA. Haven't I met *her* before somewhere?

OLIVE. Yes, at the Next Week Club; she gave a lecture the other night on books one should read, and Rebecca North replied with a few pointed remarks on "Books one should not write." Poor Naomi was completely routed.

KELD. Would she be good copy?

OLIVE. Excellent, she's a "soul"; she does her own washing up with a volume of Verlaine wedged in the soap box. She says she couldn't live without the classics, and seems to imagine that the classics couldn't live without her.

KELD. Oh do fetch her, Olive, I'll put her in a play.

OLIVE. I'm afraid she's a rather basic type , but still –

(She rises.)

KELD. Nevermind.

OLIVE. I shan't be long.

(Exit **OLIVE.***)*

KELD. Well, it's your last night of freedom, do you feel frightened?

SHEILA. Of course not, I'm thrilled.

KELD. So am I, but I'm frightened as well – terrified! I suppose it's silly nerves, but to be on the brink of a great happiness is a scarifying feeling.

SHEILA. You'll be a wreck tomorrow if you go on worrying over nothing.

KELD. Oh, no I shan't, there's not much longer to wait now, thank heaven – we've been very patient. I say, doesn't "we've" sound simply wonderful; a few months ago there wasn't any "we've" only "I've"!

SHEILA. Yes, it stands for our love and our happiness and the joy of working together and helping one another to make our way in the world. Oh, Keld darling, wouldn't it be awful if we failed!

KELD. You're getting nervous now.

SHEILA. I'm not nervous over the immediate future; I'm looking further ahead; we might be over ambitious and wreck our happiness or under ambitious and wreck our *careers*.

KELD. We must make up our minds firmly to stick to the middle way and have both happiness and careers.

SHEILA. It sounds easy but it will probably be a struggle.

KELD. Well as long as we struggle together it won't matter.

SHEILA. *(With fervour.)* Yes! That's what we must do. Struggle together. Don't lets part in thought for one minute, or even have a difference of opinion, they *are* so undermining.

KELD. *(Laughing.)* Darling, you must be reasonable. I'm afraid we shan't be able to get to the end of our married life without occasional arguments.

SHEILA. Yes, but let's keep to little ones, they're less dangerous. Oh I do love you Keld; but somehow I don't believe there is enough of the maternal in my affection; I feel that to be a good wife I should want to smooth your hair and warm your slippers and be tactful at breakfast, but I don't. I want to kiss you – and to ruffle your hair hard, not smooth it.

(She does so.)

KELD. *(Kissing her passionately.)* You're adorable, you're wonderful! I – I – Oh God! *(His words are lost in an increasingly passionate kiss.)*

SHEILA. *(Half-laughing and breaking away.)* Do stop Keld.

KELD. I like that! You ruffled my hair first.

SHEILA. I couldn't help it, it was asking to be ruffled, all sleek and flat *(She rubs her hands together.)* – and greasy.

KELD. It's the best hair wash in London – smell. *(He proffers his head.)*

SHEILA. *(Sniffing.)* Yes, it is rather nice.

KELD. If you were a proper girlish bride you'd like me to reek of tobacco and tweed, and you could call me your "grumpy daddy"; don't you think that would be awfully attractive?

(There is the noise of the outer door opening.)

SHEILA. Look out, here they come – do let them catch us embracing, they rather expect it of us – I hate disappointing people!

(They embrace.)

(Enter **OLIVE**, **NAOMI** *and* **EDMUND**. **KELD** *and* **SHEILA** *break away from one another in assumed embarrassment.)*

KELD. By Jove, I –

SHEILA. We never heard you, I –

OLIVE. Don't pretend. You know you wouldn't mind the whole world watching you kiss, you frequently do it on buses when your feelings become too much for you.

SHEILA. Olive, we only did it once, and that was outside with one old man looking on.

OLIVE. We won't argue about it now – you all know one another, at least by name, don't you? Naomi Frith-Bassington, Sheila Brandreth, Edmund Crowe, Keld Maxwell. How I loathe introducing people. Do sit down everybody and talk. I can't be entertaining tonight, it saps my vitality dreadfully having to keep a restraining hand upon Sheila's bubbling spirits. I've been terrified during the last few days that she'd suddenly scream with excitement in the street.

NAOMI. Miss Brandreth, how courageous it is of you to marry! I should never dare.

KELD. Why not?

NAOMI. Well Edmund and I realise the value of love shouldn't be fettered down by the chains of matrimony.

SHEILA. Keld and I don't intend to be fettered in any way; personally I think that the strain of living together openly would be much harder to bear. I should hate self-righteous people to look down their noses at me.

EDMUND. That sort of thing though is so trivial.

SHEILA. Trivial perhaps when you haven't got to make a success in the world, but you see we have, and we don't mean to be handicapped at the start by adverse public opinion. Also, we shall feel happier – married.

NAOMI. Of course, but that is just the horror of it, being married out of fear under those circumstances and not for love.

OLIVE. *(Laughing.)* In view of tomorrow's event, I think this is quite the most delicious argument I've ever heard.

NAOMI. You see Edmund and I are so happy, somehow I feel it my duty to try and help others be happy too.

SHEILA. Your theory is that love should be free?

NAOMI. *(Enthusiastically.)* Absolutely, free – always.

KELD. Like the National Gallery.

SHEILA. Keld.

OLIVE. Personally I agree with Sheila.

SHEILA. Then there's another point – how do you face the child problem? To me it seems terribly cruel to bring a child into the world under *any* circumstances, but to make it illegitimate as well, is surely adding unnecessary insult to injury.

NAOMI. Nowadays that sort of thing never matters; do you imagine that I should mind if I were illegitimate?

SHEILA. Perhaps not, but your son or daughter, when grown up might have different views.

    (An awkward pause.)

NAOMI. Anyhow Edmund and I are not going to have any children.

KELD. Supreme faith in a benevolent Providence must be a great comfort.

    *(**SHEILA** and **KELD** exchange a look of mutual satisfaction.)*

EDMUND. *(With an air of taking up a pre-arranged cue.)* By the way, apropos of Providence, have you read Naomi's new book *Fate's Plaything*? It came out last week.

SHEILA. No, I'm afraid I haven't yet.

NAOMI. I'll send you a copy. I should value your criticism very highly.

SHEILA. Thank you so much –

NAOMI. Of course I'm afraid in some ways it is a little outspoken, but one can't write of Bohemia without defying convention a tiny bit.

KELD. I didn't know there was any Bohemia left now.

(*Another slight pause.*)

OLIVE. Personally I've given up writing with a message to humanity in it. *Only A Shop Girl,* for instance my masterpiece – eight thousand words – firmly refused by every editor in London. Even *Fireside Fun* turned it down.

SHEILA. Fancy sending it to such an awful –

OLIVE. (*Holding up her hand.*) Don't dear, don't. I won't hear a word against *Fireside Fun*. It may not like my story, its sense may not be attuned to the pathos and yearning of *Only a Shop Girl,* but in spite of that it is a splendid little paper, it says so on the cover and it ought to know.

NAOMI. I know the editor of *Home Happiness* perhaps it –

OLIVE. No, I've sent it there, they were nicer. They said it wasn't the type of thing that they published, but that they liked my style.

EDMUND. It is heartrending to send one's work to unappreciative boors who fail to understand one's message.

(*Yet another awkward pause.*)

KELD. Would you all think it frightfully rude of me if I went home to bed now?

SHEILA. Oh Keld!

KELD. Now don't press me to stay; we're going to be together to the end of our lives and I want a good night's rest in order to face the situation with the requisite courage.

SHEILA. *(Laughing.)* You are a beast.

KELD. Well anyhow, good night, darling.

> *(He kisses her fondly.)*

SHEILA. Good night dear.

> *(He shakes hands with **NAOMI** and **EDMUND**.)*

KELD. Olive.

> *(He kisses her.)*

OLIVE. Good night Keld. Try to sleep.

> *(**KELD** laughs and goes off, followed by **SHEILA**.)*

NAOMI. I suppose we really ought to be going too.

OLIVE. Oh no, it's quite early yet.

NAOMI. *(Rising.)* But as it's your last night with Miss Brandreth I'm sure you'll want to be alone and talk! It must be a great wrench parting.

OLIVE. I shall miss her dreadfully.

EDMUND. *(Shaking hands with **OLIVE**.)* Good night, Mrs Kennedy; thank you so much for letting us come up.

OLIVE. Not at all. I hope you'll come again, and cheer my loneliness.

NAOMI. We should love to.

> *(They go to the door and meet **SHEILA** re-entering.)*

Oh Miss Brandreth, I wish you all the happiness in the world; nothing can ever matter in life if people really love each other.

SHEILA. Thank you very much. You will come and see us soon, won't you?

EDMUND. Good night, all my best wishes too.

SHEILA. Thank you, you're both very kind.

> *(Exit* **NAOMI** *and* **EDMUND.***)*

> *(***OLIVE** *sees them out and then returns.)*

> *(***SHEILA** *sinks into a chair. She continues...)*

How nice it is of people to be so kind, and how perfectly awful to have to keep saying "Good night – Thank You", "Good night – Thank you so much", "Thank you – good night."

OLIVE. It is difficult to keep from being monotonous; I suppose we really ought to manage it by inflection. "*Good* night, thank you. Good *night*, thank you."

SHEILA. If I hear those words again I shall go raving mad.

OLIVE. I feel that the moment has now arrived for us to say a few sentimental words to each other and retire firmly to bed.

SHEILA. Oh, Olive, isn't it awful, the last evening in this flat together! I'm so miserable.

OLIVE. *(Laughing.)* Miserable! If only you could see yourself at the moment, so bubbling over with happiness that you can hardly speak. You're going to have a nice strong husband to honour and obey you, and endless love and romance, and – the thought of it makes me quite maudlin – I shall be left alone, Sheila, all alone, when you are giving your gorgeous dinner parties and receptions and standing at the top of the staircase superbly dressed receiving your guests, I –

SHEILA. As we don't intend to entertain our guests in the bathroom, dear, it would be simpler to receive them in the hall – the staircase is *very* narrow.

OLIVE. I was referring to a time when, as a result of the vast fortunes earned by you both, you have a mansion in Park Lane.

SHEILA. There are few things I should dislike more. I've no wish to live among the lost ten tribes.

OLIVE. Seriously, darling I do *hate* you're going.

SHEILA. I can't think why you're adopting this depressingly hopeless attitude just as if a little thing like marriage could ever make any difference to us.

OLIVE. I wasn't thinking of that.

SHEILA. Then?

OLIVE. *(Suddenly.)* Sheila, I'm going to do a dreadful thing just as a sort of salve to my conscience. I'm going to deliver a warning to you, and…so please try to be serious.

SHEILA. All right, dear.

OLIVE. Well, to begin with, I have a pet theory. I'm sensible enough to keep it in a cage, but still it lives on fat pieces of experience, and when there's the least likelihood of trouble it sings. It's singing now.

SHEILA. You're not exactly cheering tonight, are you?

OLIVE. Worse to come, dear. In the course of conversation I'm going to tell you that "it's all for your own good" and that "it's my duty as a friend to speak out, etc." If suitably encouraged I might also be induced to say that "as you are alone in the world" –

SHEILA. *(Interrupting.)* You're being flippant now.

OLIVE. This is my theory: when two brilliant egoists marry, unless one of them is prepared to sacrifice certain things, there is bound to be trouble.

SHEILA. What kind of things?

OLIVE. Either you or Keld will have to sacrifice a certain amount of personality; no two people of your intellectual abilities could live together for long without getting on one another's nerves, it's a psychological impossibility.

SHEILA. Do you class our intellects as equals?

OLIVE. Far from it, dear, you are much the cleverer of the two, and because of that I prophesy that you will be the one to give in.

SHEILA. Olive, I don't agree. I love Keld and he loves me really deep down, therefore being the clever man that he is, he won't want to give up one particle of either my work *or* my personality.

OLIVE. I can only remark with gentle emphasis that I have been married before, and you haven't.

SHEILA. You don't understand, Keld and I are different, we've both knocked about a good lot and we realise the value of real love and comradeship; instead of jarring each other as you say we will, we shall encourage one another's intellects and work. We've talked it all over, we're not marrying blindly, on the impulse of a sudden infatuation. We're marrying as lovers, I grant you, but our love is mental as well as physical. I love Keld's dear intelligence as much as my own, and he is the same.

OLIVE. That is the one weak spot dear. You can never be sure that he is the same; he may appear to be at first, men often do, but it will, in all probability wear off quite soon. I only want to warn you for your own good.

SHEILA. You've said it, you perfect lamb, you've said it. I know it's for my own good, but don't let's be serious anymore, it's my last night of singleness, and any woman who has psychological discussions on her wedding eve deserves to be unhappy. Keld was so wonderful all through lunch today, the perfect sheepish groom, he kept on pressing my hand under the table and saying, "little wife soon to be." Wasn't it rather adorable of him?

OLIVE. Yes, it was rather.

SHEILA. I gazed coyly at him and tried to look as though I'd never written anything but laundry and library lists.

OLIVE. Wouldn't it be awful if you had ultimately to give up your writing altogether?

SHEILA. What do you mean?

OLIVE. You may have to.

SHEILA. But I couldn't give it up, you don't understand – it's my greatest happiness. As I write now I'm providing myself with a key, and when I'm old and have no future at all, I shall use it to unlock the door of the past.

OLIVE. Yes dear, but –

SHEILA. I mean to make Keld work as well. Olive, he's going to be great, you can see by the stuff he's done already, and he's quite young yet. I want to be at the first night of his first play. Just think of the thrill of it. All London sailing in determined to be critical and destructive, and they won't get the chance because it will be a success, a tremendous artistic success, and I shall be sitting there saying to myself every word of it, awaiting the laughs and applause.

OLIVE. Do you think his work really is clever?

SHEILA. Yes, I do; he has a wonderful sense of the dramatic and his dialogue is exceedingly witty. He may fail a little in construction, but that won't matter a bit if he shows real sincerity.

OLIVE. *(Dubiously.)* No, I suppose not.

SHEILA. Do you know I believe you dislike Keld.

OLIVE. Don't be absurd Sheila, I'm as fond as I could ever be of a man who is taking you away. I shall be extraordinarily lonely without you.

SHEILA. My lamb!

(*She kisses her.*)

I'll take jolly good care you're not without me – much.

OLIVE. You won't be able to help it for the first few – years.

SHEILA. You were going to say weeks! I saw it coming. (*She looks at the photograph in a big frame on the table.*) He's such a darling.

OLIVE. (*Acidly.*) He's sweet.

SHEILA. I'm sure you're against him for something Olive, I just wish I could find out what it is.

OLIVE. I've nothing against him at all – really, but somehow – well, to begin with he has talent, we know, but nothing compared to you; coupled with that he has, if anything, a bit more of a temper than you. As you know I place a very high value on your brain. You're going to be great if you work; Keld can never be great.

SHEILA. But Olive –

OLIVE. No, let me go on. He may be successful, wildly successful, but not great, and my one all-absorbing fear is that you in time will become so enthralled and interested in his work that you'll allow yours to go to the wall. He'll have your brain as well as his own with which to write.

SHEILA. He doesn't need it and as for letting my work go, it's absurd. A few minutes ago you said you were afraid that I should give up writing voluntarily; now you say that I shall merge my brain with Keld's. I tell you firmly I shall do neither. I love him too much to give in to him.

OLIVE. You'll probably give in to him too much to love him.

SHEILA. If you make one more epigram Olive, I shall break something valuable.

OLIVE. You can't dear, it's a furnished flat.

SHEILA. You think I shall stop loving him after a time, but you're wrong, I won't. For the last few years I've written cynical criticisms of other people's love stories, burlesqued romance and laughed at passion until at last love, romance and passion have risen up and jumped on me hard, just to show what a fool I've been! Keld may die or run away with another woman forgetting me altogether, but I shall go on loving him, whatever happens. I shall probably go through hell later on, but I shall love him to the last day of my life.

> *(Pause.)*

OLIVE. Perhaps so dear. It's an ill wind that blows somebody…something. I wish I could get that right, I've never been able to yet.

SHEILA. I hope you never will. It's a most irritating remark.

OLIVE. Sometimes it's such a relief to fall back on the commonplaces. "Marriage is a lottery" there's another. Shall we go to bed now?

SHEILA. I suppose we'd better, but I know I shan't sleep.

OLIVE. I've placed a copy of *Marriage* by HG Wells at your bedside. You'll sleep soundly I assure you. After you.

SHEILA. Very well.

> *(She exits.)*

OLIVE. "Little wife soon to be."

> *(**OLIVE** laughs.)*

> *(Curtain.)*

ACT TWO

(Six months later.)

(The study of **KELD MAXWELL**'s *house in Belgravia. As the lights come up* **KELD** *is at his table typing busily.)*

(There is a knock at the door.)

KELD. Come in.

(Another knock.)

Come in!

*(***BURRAGE*** enters.)*

BURRAGE. Excuse me Sir, but will you be in for dinner tonight?

KELD. I've just finished breakfast.

BURRAGE. I want to know what to order in, Sir.

KELD. Burrage, in well-managed houses dinner is always on the table at the correct time, irrespective of whether the master happens to be in or not.

BURRAGE. That wouldn't be very economical, Sir.

KELD. Burrage, the various intricacies of household economy are not as interesting to me as they are to you. I have other, if not greater or at least equally important work to attend to; would you be kind enough to discuss the dinner problem with your mistress?

BURRAGE. The mistress said she was going to be busy all morning, Sir.

KELD. Well I'm busy too; if necessary we'll go without dinner.

BURRAGE. There's no need for that Sir, there's always cold mutton from yesterday.

KELD. That is a source of immeasurable comfort to me.

BURRAGE. If I warmed it up, I might get in some vegetables and make a casserole of it.

KELD. Doubtless there are no limits to what you might do with the mutton, Burrage. Please don't mention the subject again in my hearing – I'm exceedingly busy.

BURRAGE. *(Injured.)* I only thought it best, Sir, to consult you.

KELD. You were perfectly right, and I assure you I feel most flattered by the attention. However, I'm mentally incapable of grappling with the subject. Will you leave me now, please, Burrage?

BURRAGE. I'm very sorry, Sir –

KELD. Don't apologize, after all it's your profession and only natural that you should wish to talk about it. If I discussed dramatic construction with you, you'd be bored stiff.

BURRAGE. Would I, Sir?

KELD. I'm certain you would. And I feel the same about mutton. *Do* go away now Burrage.

BURRAGE. I couldn't very well walk away Sir, when you was talking. It wouldn't have been respectful.

   (**BURRAGE** *exits.*)

   (**KELD** *returns to his typing for a few moments, then a loud ring of the doorbell is heard,* *followed by a rat-a-tat-tat of the door knocker.* **KELD** *goes to the door and listens, he hears the sound of voices outside and then finally another knock at the study door.)*

KELD. Come in for God's sake.

*(Re-enter **BURRAGE**.)*

BURRAGE. Miss Raymond to see you Sir.

KELD. Miss who?

BURRAGE. Miss Raymond; Ruby Raymond I think she said, Sir.

KELD. Oh. Show her in.

BURRAGE. Yes Sir.

*(Before **BURRAGE** can do so, **RUBY RAYMOND** laden with sables, enters.)*

Miss Ruby Raymond.

*(Exit **BURRAGE**.)*

RUBY. Oh please forgive me Mr Maxwell for coming *so* early but I wanted to catch you before you went out.

KELD. I'm delighted Miss Raymond, do sit down, won't you?

RUBY. Thanks.

(She sits and loosens her sables.)

I'm not generally up at this time, you know, still it's a nice change to be out before eleven for once.

KELD. Have a cigarette?

RUBY. No thanks, I never dare smoke before lunch because of my voice. I mustn't take up too much of *your* morning. I'm sure you must be fearfully busy.

RUBY. I only came round to ask you when they're really going to start rehearsals. I wouldn't ask Charlie Baker, he'd want to know what I wanted to know for. Managers are awful – so inquisitive. As a matter of fact, between you and me, I'm going down to Frinton for a few days.

KELD. I think they intend to begin next Monday.

RUBY. That gives me nearly a week. You won't let on where I am, will you? You know what Charlie is.

KELD. Is he anything beyond being a business manager?

RUBY. Well he's got a bit of a crush on me, ever since he met me at Dodie's party. D'you know Dodie? He gives jolly good parties.

KELD. I'm afraid I don't.

RUBY. He's a nice boy. Anyhow Charlie won't leave me alone now. I did think I was going to get away from all that sort of thing when I left musical comedy.

KELD. Do you know Miss Raymond, I'm sadly afraid you'll never get away from "that sort of thing" and even if you did, I'm sure you'd hate it.

RUBY. *(Laughing.)* Oh God! I keep forgetting. I'm talking to an author. You get me all the time – it's uncanny. Between you and me, Charlie's gaga over me.

KELD. Yes, I noticed something of the sort when I saw you both at the reading last week. Was it through him you got the engagement?

RUBY. Yes. I've been wanting to go into straight stuff for ages and he fixed it all up with Samson for me.

KELD. I'm glad you're making your first plunge into legitimate drama in my first play; it gives us a sort of bond in common, doesn't it?

RUBY. By the way, what's Irene Harrison like?

KELD. On or off?

RUBY. Off. I'd like to know what I'm in for before we start.

KELD. I believe she's very charming. I've only met her twice. Of course she'll be marvelous in the part, tho' I'm afraid she's a little inclined to be unsympathetic.

RUBY. Now that's exactly what I say, and she doesn't dress smartly enough – too…bitty.

KELD. I shall be very interested to see how you and she get on together.

RUBY. Oh, I shall be perfectly natural with her. If she gets jealous though… I can't help it, can I?

KELD. Do you think she will?

RUBY. Oh you never know. Look what a swine Cissy Neville was after the first night of *Kiss Granny*; we'd been such pals too, and just because I'd made a success she stuck my photograph up in the scullery next to Horatio Bottomley.

KELD. *(Amused.)* That was real malice.

RUBY. And the fuss she made about dressing rooms; not that I minded being put up on the second floor; but it was hard luck on the guards having to tramp up all those stairs after they'd been fighting for us and everything.

KELD. I see that you possess the true patriotic spirit.

RUBY. Now you're being sarcastic, I know you are! Still I never thought you'd be so nice. Between you and me, I was a bit frightened of coming to see you. I don't quite know why I did it either – half to spite Charlie and half to be on good terms with the author.

KELD. *(Roaring with laughter.)* You really are an amazing person. Anyhow, you've succeeded in one half; I can't answer for Charlie's feelings in the matter.

RUBY. I don't care what he thinks really.

KELD. Why do you encourage him?

RUBY. I don't, beyond letting him take me out to lunch every day. He keeps on telling me of nice little places he knows in Soho, but I'm quite happy at Claridge's; there's something so country about Claridge's.

KELD. Yes, there is. One feels that even the waiters are the sons of retired colonels.

RUBY. *(Rising.)* Well I really must be going now. I've trespassed on your time too much as it is.

KELD. *(Hurriedly.)* Please don't dream of going yet, you're not trespassing a bit. I love you being here.

RUBY. *(Sitting down again.)* Oh well, I'm sure I don't know what Charlie'd say; he'd think I was getting round you to write in new bits for me.

KELD. Well aren't you?

RUBY. *(Laughing.)* Exit designing actress, crushed by a blunt question. Yes perhaps that's what I *do* want; after all it would be nice to make a big success, and my part's not very large.

KELD. As a matter of fact, I am writing you an entirely new scene. They didn't like the end of the second act as it was, so now I'm going to make you come in and tell Sylvia everything.

RUBY. Lovely! Is it dramatic?

KELD. Yes of course but it's humourous too. I believe it will play very well.

RUBY. Irene Harrison plays Sylvia doesn't she?

KELD. Yes.

RUBY. Oh God!

KELD. Why, "Oh God?"

RUBY. I don't know she looks the kind of woman who'd cut in on one's laughs.

KELD. I don't think she will, you mustn't be too prejudiced against her before you start, it will only end in trouble.

RUBY. Do go on telling me about the new scene. Have you finished it?

KELD. Oh no, I've only done the rough outline, but in it you decide to give Jack up and come and ask Sylvia's forgiveness; of course it's a bit sloppy, but still –

RUBY. I think it sounds perfectly wonderful. I can't imagine how people can write. I'd give anything to be able to, like you do.

KELD. But you can sing and dance and act instead.

RUBY. You haven't seen me act properly yet; I haven't had the chance.

KELD. I'd love to write a part for you exactly as you are.

RUBY. The censor'd go off the deep end if you did.

KELD. Then I should write it very carefully.

RUBY. What I want is something really dramatic; you know, having a child and not finding the father until the last act. I want a bit of solid realism.

KELD. You ought to do some repertory work.

RUBY. I can't speak Lancashire well enough, but still, anything to get into real straight stuff – I'm fed to the teeth with musical comedy.

KELD. Are you satisfied with this part?

RUBY. Oh, rather, even though it isn't the lead; it will be such a relief not having the chorus dodging behind me.

(**RUBY** *suddenly laughs loudly.*)

KELD. What is it now?

RUBY. Oh, I've just "got" myself, that's all – *I* should be haughty about the chorus – I was in it myself two years ago!

(**RUBY** *rises.*)

RUBY. I really must go now, I've got to pack for Frinton. You're sure they won't begin 'til Monday?

(**KELD** *helps her with her furs.*)

KELD. Yes, quite.

RUBY. Will you come and have tea with me one day?

KELD. I'd simply love to.

RUBY. Well, do and I'll try to make you write in a bit more for me, but you won't make me out too hard, will you? I'm not a bit really, you know – do make me nice to what's-his-name in the last act, even if I am chucking him. I always believe in keeping on being sweet to people whatever happens, it does them in so damned well. I shall finish with Charlie soon, but I shan't cut him or anything like that – too much a giveaway. I shall just behave as though nothing had happened.

KELD. I hope nothing has.

(**KELD** *rings the bell.*)

RUBY. Oh well, you know what I mean.

KELD. When do you intend to deal the final blow to his happiness?

RUBY. Oh not 'til after the first night; he arranges all my press interviews for me, and it would be silly to throw away good advertisement deliberately.

KELD. Can it be, Miss Raymond, that you have a mercenary mind?

RUBY. You'd have a mercenary mind if you were with Charlie for long. You won't let on about Frinton, will you?

KELD. I won't mention it at all.

RUBY. Promise?

KELD. Promise.

(**BURRAGE** *enters.*)

RUBY. He'd be livid with me, and you know what Jews are like when they're roused.

KELD. They very seldom are though.

RUBY. If it wasn't that Charlie had a wife already I should've been dragged to the Synagogue ages ago. I believe he's trying to divorce her or something – just as if I'd ever marry him. Between you and me I like a man to be a bit more up and doing. Charlie grovels too much, but still he *is* the Business Manager! Good-bye. See you on Monday.

(*Exit* **RUBY** *followed by* **BURRAGE**.)

(**KELD** *left alone laughs to himself and then sits down and commences to work again.*)

(**SHEILA** *enters.*)

KELD. Oh Damn!

SHEILA. What's the matter dear?

KELD. I've been trying all blessed morning to get this scene *done* and there have been nothing but interruptions and disturbances.

SHEILA. Well you often disturb *me* at my work; anyhow, I wanted a pencil, you've taken practically every one in the house.

(*She takes a pencil from the tray.*)

KELD. Not that one, it's the best.

SHEILA. (*Laughing.*) Don't you think I deserve the best, darling? After all, you have the comfortable study to work in *and* the typewriter.

KELD. Why don't you buy one for yourself?

(**SHEILA** *leans over and kisses* **KELD**.)

SHEILA. Don't be grumpy, there's a lamb.

KELD. If I were allowed to write in peace, I shouldn't ever want to be grumpy.

SHEILA. You're hardly ever disturbed, really, you know – just this morning perhaps once or twice – you mustn't be unreasonable.

(She sniffs.)

What a funny scent. Who's been here?

KELD. Miss Ruby Raymond.

SHEILA. Who's she?

KELD. You know perfectly well. I told you the other day, she's playing the tart in my play.

SHEILA. Well, I'm sure she'll make a success of it if she continues to use this scent. By the way, will you be in for dinner?

KELD. No, I shall dine in the Sahara Desert tonight.

SHEILA. Why the sarcasm? Are you upset over something?

KELD. I'm being driven to a frenzy by that question; constant repetition of a thing is apt to grate on one's nerves.

SHEILA. I haven't mentioned it before.

KELD. Burrage has. *Twice* already this morning.

SHEILA. I hope you weren't rude Keld, excellent servants are quite difficult to find.

KELD. Burrage would be even more excellent without bothering me.

SHEILA. You're being terribly disagreeable and rude this morning.

KELD. I tell you I haven't been rude. You can't expect me to work when I'm worried every few minutes by inane domestic questions, surely that is rather more your department than mine?

SHEILA. No it's not, I have to work too. Why don't you lock the door?

KELD. Because if I did Burrage would bang until I opened it. You shut yourself in your room all day and lock the door.

SHEILA. Now Keld darling, *don't* be tiresome. You know I'm working hard as well and have to lock myself in; anyone would think that my sole mission in life was to arrange your meals with Burrage.

KELD. If you mention Burrage's name again I'll – I'll yell the place down.

SHEILA. Really, you are childish, making such a fuss over trifles, here you are, surrounded by everything you want, in a cosy room where you can write in absolute comfort, and all you do is get nervy and irritated over nothing at all. You must pull yourself together, darling.

KELD. But it is so awful, just when I'm concentrating on an important scene – to have my thoughts wrenched away to mutton. Why, the word "mutton" is enough to damn anyone's inspiration.

SHEILA. You couldn't have been concentrating very hard with Ruby what's-her-name here.

KELD. I was concentrating before she came and her name is Raymond.

SHEILA. I doubt that, it's probably Blagins or Winterbottom or something terrible. Raymond doesn't sound genuine to me, anyhow why not blame her for disturbing you instead of Burrage.

KELD. There you go again, back to Burrage! Hadn't we better give the dear thing notice before we land in the divorce courts?

SHEILA. Oh Keld, aren't we fools? We were actually getting quite heated.

KELD. I wasn't. It was only airy badinage.

SHEILA. Yes you were, come on, admit it like a darling. So was I. I could have hit you several times.

(She kisses him.)

It's been one of the most tiresome mornings I've ever known. Everything's gone wrong: no pencils, bad egg at breakfast, you and Burrage, that irritating letter from Naomi asking for our subscriptions to her club. No wonder we're both fractious. Let's unsay everything since we got up, and start all over again.

KELD. Angel, we will!

(He kisses her.)

I love you more than ever after we've just been bickering; it gives a sort of relish.

SHEILA. I hate it. I'm quite happy without relish. Don't let's bicker any more, it's a terrible waste of time.

KELD. All right, we won't. I was only trying to make the best of our silliness. How's *The Shadow Show* going?

SHEILA. Not frightfully well; I've only done two chapters. I'm thrilled with the idea, but somehow it's difficult to get really started. Wouldn't it be wonderful to be able to just think out a novel and see it lying complete in front of you without the terrible strain of writing it?

KELD. Published, or just proofs?

SHEILA. Oh, proofs, so that you could make a fuss of correcting them, and say how hard working you were.

KELD. Sometimes I wish we neither of us wrote at all.

SHEILA. Why, dear? We're awfully happy.

KELD. Yes, but somehow, oh I don't know, it would be rather nice to go up to the city every day and do commonplace monotonous work, and lunch at the same place, with the same people and catch the same train back in the evening, to be greeted by you, perfectly dull and sweet, full of thrilling little bits of news about the model vacuum cleaner and how you snapped back to the cook when she gave notice. Think of the wonderful tranquility of having no temperament or intellect.

SHEILA. Would you like me to be like that now?

KELD. My darling, don't be absurd. Do you think I could go on loving you for a moment without your dear intelligence and brain?

SHEILA. I sometimes wonder, that's all.

KELD. Well I wish you wouldn't; it never does any good to wonder about those sort of things.

SHEILA. All right dear, I won't. Now I must go and do some more work; I'm sure you're dying to as well. I'll read you my two chapters after lunch.

KELD. Oh well then before we both start again I want to read you this bit of the second act.

SHEILA. *(Without enthusiasm.)* We've wasted an awful lot of time already.

KELD. Of course, if you don't want to hear it…

SHEILA. It isn't that I don't want to, but it's nearly half-past twelve now and we've hardly done anything this morning. Why not read it after lunch when I read mine.

KELD. I don't suppose I shall feel in the mood then.

SHEILA. *(Flopping impatiently into a chair.)* Oh go on then.

KELD. Well as a matter of fact I haven't actually written it yet. I just wanted to know if you approve of the idea, the end of the second act, you know. Instead of having Rose, the tart, truculent all through, I'm going to make her apologise to Sylvia rather pathetically for everything –

SHEILA. But she never would –

KELD. Why not?

SHEILA. Certainly not the type you've written. You'd have to alter the whole character to make her do that. No girl who had –

KELD. But my dear Sheila, I don't see why tarts shouldn't be apologetic as well as anyone else.

SHEILA. Yes, but *not* the character you've drawn; she's much too hard, also she's supposed to hate Sylvia. There's no earthly reason for her suddenly to turn repentant and nice, it's psychologically wrong.

KELD. It isn't psychologically wrong. Why, Ruby Raymond was raving about it just now. She said that –

SHEILA. Of course if you go to ex-chorus girls for criticisms, why ask me?

KELD. Don't be silly, Sheila.

SHEILA. It's you who are being silly, quoting Ruby Raymond to me. We'll think out something different for the end of each act after lunch.

KELD. I don't want anything different. I'm quite satisfied with this.

SHEILA. Are you *actually* pretending to know more about women than I do?

KELD. I'm not pretending at all. You being a woman yourself, are much too down on your sex; I regard you all impartially with the eye of an observer.

SHEILA. Yes, like standing outside of Buckingham Palace and trying to make an inventory of the furniture.

KELD. Not at all. I've had lots of opportunities of studying women.

SHEILA. You may have had plenty of opportunities but there's nothing to prove you've taken advantage of them. Your writing certainly doesn't.

KELD. It's silly to be catty about my writing, just because we happen to disagree.

SHEILA. I wasn't in the least catty. I merely say that your women aren't good. No man, unless he's abnormal, can ever really get a grip on the feminine mind, and you're not a bit abnormal.

KELD. I'm afraid darling, you're rather talking through your hat; heaps of perfectly normal men have written brilliantly about women.

SHEILA. Perhaps but only up to a certain point. Of course you haven't reached that point with Rose, she's an obvious type, she'd never, never, never, become a charming sympathetic character after all her beastliness. You know perfectly well I'm right now, don't you?

KELD. No I don't. I like Rose in spite of her beastliness. I feel that given the opportunity she *would* be repentant.

SHEILA. If you don't like my criticism you shouldn't have asked for it.

KELD. You're only being destructive because you weren't keen to hear what I'd done. You read your stuff to me on every possible occasion and always get impatient when I try to read you mine.

SHEILA. *(Angrily.)* It isn't fair of you to say things like that Keld, and it's not true. I love your work, and I'm always ready to take an interest, that's why I criticise. If you can't stand the criticism you'll never get anywhere. You think you know all there is to know about women, and yet you really know nothing about them at all except superficialities. Look at the heroine of that one act play you did last month –

KELD. That's it, drag that up again. I admitted I was wrong then; I couldn't do more. I know one thing about women, and that is –

SHEILA. Don't lose your temper, it's so foolish.

KELD. *(Furiously.)* I'm not losing my temper, but I shall if, whenever we have an argument, you can't keep from raking up all the things we said weeks ago.

SHEILA. I didn't rake up anything, I merely pointed out that –

KELD. That I happened really to be in the wrong for once. I know you'll never let me forget it; that's typical of a woman.

SHEILA. And just because I give you an honest criticism of your work you get childish and rude.

KELD. If you had only stayed up in your own room this morning and not come down and disturbed me, we should both have been saved all this aimless bickering.

SHEILA. You said you liked bickering just now because it was relish. Anyhow I had no pencil. You take jolly good care to have everything you want round you when you want to work. You grab all the writing necessities, leaving me *none*. Have you ever been without a pen or pencil for one moment since we've been married?

KELD. Oh, for heaven's sake don't harp on the beastly pencils; buy hundreds and hundreds and hundreds and give me the bill. I'll pay it willingly – anything, anything for peace.

SHEILA. *(Sarcastically.)* My dear Keld, can it be that you are beginning to see yourself in the picture as a henpecked husband?

KELD. I'm only playing up to your marvellous impersonation of a nagging wife – it's very stupid of you to do it. I have to finish off this play to make money for us both, and all you do is to –

SHEILA. Anyone would think that you were the only one who earned anything. On what have we been living for the last month? Cheques for my short stories and occasional royalties for my last book.

KELD. Oh, I know all that, I'm only a beginner, but what you say only proves the necessity of my earning a *lot* quite soon. Even your brilliant short stories won't go on forever; therefore, Sheila *dear*, would you be kind enough to leave me to my work now?

SHEILA. No, I won't leave you to your work; you won't be able to write a word after all this squabbling and neither shall I. I'll go upstairs and think of the beastly things I might have said to you and regret not having said them, and you would do the same down here. That's not good for our future happiness. If we can't get on together without this eternal jarring we'd better face it. It's dangerous to leave little unfinished quarrels lying around the place like loose ends; they might join together and wreck our lives later on.

KELD. What do you intend to do? Have a pitched battle?

SHEILA. It's serious, and you know it. For the past three months we've had absurd nagging arguments like this one on an average of about four times a week. Of course, we always make it up in the end, but that doesn't put things right; we break out again in a day or two over some trivial irritation and work ourselves up into tempers, and say malicious things to each other – all for nothing! That only proves that there is something radically wrong with either one or both of us, and the sooner we find out, the better.

KELD. I quite agree but how are we to do it? I quite realise the folly of sparring and hurling caustic epithets at each other? I've known it for quite a long time. I've vowed frequently that never, never, never, shall an unkind word pass my lips again, but it's all to no avail; an hour later I find myself embroiled in a fierce verbal skirmish from which it is impossible to escape without considerable loses on both sides.

SHEILA. Our temperaments and talents are too much alike. It would be better if you were an engineer or a stockbroker.

KELD. On the contrary, it would be infinitely worse; you'd not take the slightest interest in my work, and I'd have no toleration or understanding of yours.

SHEILA. Do you honestly think that we're interested in each other's work now?

KELD. Yes, of course we are.

SHEILA. I'm not so sure. I know we try very hard, but I don't feel that there is any real interest there. There's a certain element of jealousy which stands in our way. I need to discover what the trouble is. We're not happy together Keld, don't you realise it? We're not happy.

(She almost cries.)

KELD. *(Comforting her.)* It isn't as bad as that, I *know* these rows are only silly trivialities.

SHEILA. No they're not, they're not. They go deeper down, and if we don't stop in time we – oh don't you see what I mean? Something horrible will happen, we shall separate or –

KELD. Darling, I think all married couples with any temperament have squabbles, it's only natural and as for being jealous of one another – why that's absurd. You're wonderful and helpful to me, and I try to be the same to you. I love every word you write I –

SHEILA. *(Slowly.)* You said all that last week when we'd just made up a quarrel, don't you remember?

KELD. Yes, perhaps but –

SHEILA. And you'll say it again next week and we shall kiss and be frightfully in love until the *next* time after that.

KELD. Sheila darling you're worrying over nothing.

SHEILA. I'm not worrying over nothing. I'm worrying over our happiness; I'd sacrifice anything, anything for that. You don't see what I mean, but you've got to understand, you *must*! I love you now Keld, even more than when we married, and you love me, but each petty argument and disagreement we have will undermine that love a little more and one day it will stop in one of us, not both, no two people ever stop loving at the same time, there's always one left to be miserable. That's what these little rows lead us to, and they mustn't, they mustn't they've got to stop dead.

KELD. Perhaps if we controlled our tempers a bit more –

SHEILA. It's the feeling behind the temper that counts. Control is all very well, but there oughtn't to be anything *to* control. I tell you there's something wrong and you won't understand. I'm frightened, terribly frightened of the future. There's something lacking; perhaps it's a domestic tie we need, some sort of bond in common other than our work.

KELD. We have Burrage.

SHEILA. I don't want any humour now darling, so be a lamb and curb it. I'm quite serious and I *do* so want you to be serious too.

KELD. What is it you want to discuss? Our respective mental disturbances? A quick plunge into the treacherous pool of psychoanalysis?

SHEILA. You know very well what I mean. You're treating everything I say facetiously, and it's neither clever nor amusing, in fact it's horrid. You may be a young dramatist with an "elfin sense of humour" or imagine that you are handling your wife's hysteria with the masterful touch of a man who knows women through and through, but you're not, Keld, you're making me hate you.

KELD. My dear girl, if it's a usual failing among lady would-be-novelists to wallow in long intimate discussions about their inner lives, heaven preserve me from them.

SHEILA. Their dislike of your conceit will preserve you from them much more effectively than heaven.

KELD. Conceit? That's new, I've been accused this morning of childishness, rudeness, unintelligence, and flippancy – soon there won't be anything left to call me.

SHEILA. You flatter yourself.

KELD. It becomes necessary when my own wife fails so lamentably to appreciate my virtues.

SHEILA. If these are your virtues one can only wonder what you think of as your vices.

KELD. What a pity there isn't a stenographer here to take all this down in shorthand; it would make an excellent scene in a domestic comedy.

SHEILA. *(Losing control.)* Keld, there are times when I could kill you –

(There is a knock at the door.)

KELD. Come in.

(Enter **BURRAGE**.*)*

BURRAGE. I'm sorry to bother you again Sir, but will you be in for lunch?

KELD. I have some interesting news for you, Burrage. I intend to give up my career as a dramatist and devote myself entirely to a life of domesticity. I shall certainly be in for lunch. We will have a ragout of yesterday's mutton with sea kale and *soufflé* potatoes, we will also have –

SHEILA. *(Controlling herself with an effort.)* The master is only joking Burrage.

KELD. *(Rudely.)* I was speaking to Burrage, Sheila, don't interrupt. As I was saying after the mutton we'll have Apple Charlotte.

BURRAGE. There aren't any apples Sir.

KELD. Well go out and buy some.

BURRAGE. It's not my place to run errands, Sir, if you'd told –

KELD. I don't want to be argued with Burrage, go out and get those apples at once.

BURRAGE. I take me orders from the mistress Sir.

KELD. *(Angrily.)* On the contrary you take your orders from –

SHEILA. *(Very quietly.)* There is no need for you to get any apples Burrage, the master doesn't understand the amount of work you have to do or he wouldn't ask any more of you. You may go now.

BURRAGE. Thank you Ma'am.

*(***BURRAGE*** exits.)*

KELD. What do you mean by making me look a fool in front of Burrage?

SHEILA. *(Coldly.)* I think you must be taking leave of your senses.

KELD. Now understand me, Sheila –

SHEILA. *(Going toward the door.)* I've no intention of even trying to understand you, until you learn to behave yourself.

KELD. *(Standing in front of the door.)* I think it would be wiser to finish the little argument now, while we're in the mood.

SHEILA. Keld, let me leave.

KELD. No.

SHEILA. Are you mad?

KELD. No, at the moment I feel particularly sane.

> (**SHEILA** *goes to open the door and he seizes her arm, twisting it slightly and pushing her into a chair.*)

SHEILA. You hurt my arm.

KELD. That was your own fault.

SHEILA. I wonder if I'll be able to love you again after this.

KELD. That is beside the point –

SHEILA. No Keld it isn't –

KELD. I have only one desire at the moment and that is to impress upon you the extreme folly of making me look ridiculous before the servants. I won't have it. I put up with a lot, slovenly meals, eternal disturbances when I'm trying to work, utter lack of enthusiasm for anything I do, all merely because my wife happens to write herself, and has such a relatively high opinion of the feminine intellect that she –

SHEILA. If you possessed a little more feminine intellect yourself you'd realise that you are wrecking the future happiness of us both by this insufferable behaviour.

KELD. I think our mutual happiness has been drifting toward disaster for so long that any slight assistance from me would only hasten the inevitable.

SHEILA. Keld, please, please let's stop. Let me out of this room. We don't really mean all the horrible things we've said. Please let me go.

KELD. We must have this out, one of us must surrender.

SHEILA. *(With apprehension.)* Surrender? Surrender what?

KELD. Just give in. You're trying to beat me. It's impossible to go on living and writing in a constant atmosphere of antagonism.

SHEILA. It isn't true, there isn't any antagonism.

KELD. You're lying Sheila. You got angry because I wouldn't take you seriously, well I didn't want to because I realised what the consequences would be if I did. Now though? Damn the consequences. I'm willing to face facts, the principal one being that you're jealous of my writing.

SHEILA. Ha!

KELD. You hated me having a play accepted, I *know* you did. You like being the brilliant young novelist encouraging her moderately talented husband, and all your friends would smile and say, "Isn't Sheila Brandreth sweet to devote so much time to him? You can see her hand in all the stuff he writes; I'm so glad they're happy together, but of course with her intelligence she knows how to manage him." Well I'm sorry our married life hasn't quite come up to your expectations. I'm afraid I'm moving up too quickly for you. I know –

SHEILA. *(Furiously.)* Every word you speak is untrue. You conceited vile beast. *I* jealous of your work? *I* who from the first have done nothing but encourage and help you – why if I wasn't so utterly, wretchedly disappointed in *you,* I'd *laugh,* yes *laugh* but I can't, I can't – *(She breaks down.)*

KELD. Sheila, I'm sorry, I didn't quite mean what I said –

SHEILA. *(Pushing him away.)* Don't touch me, don't come near me – not now. For once you've gone too far – I'm finished; it was all wrong, we should never have married, however much in love we *thought* we were. Olive warned me, and it's come true. We're like two rats in a trap, fighting, fighting, fighting. You need a commonplace, domesticated wife with no brain and boundless open-mouthed appreciation for every mortal thing you do; someone who would hang on your words and convince you all the time of your incredible brilliance, the sort of woman who could be tactful when you are fractious and upset, and affectionate when you felt in the mood for it, which would be in the evening after a well-cooked and well-ordered dinner, and you'd stroke her hair and dole out a few well-chosen words of praise; not too many for fear of making her conceited, and there would never be a single moment in the day or night when you wouldn't be absolutely, unconditionally satisfied with yourself. With a larger mind you'd be a brute – but you're too contemptible and weak even for that.

KELD. Shut up! Shut up! Shut up!

(He tries to put his hand over her mouth.)

(She slaps his face furiously. He staggers back.)

SHEILA. Go away! Go away! Go away!

(He stares at her. Is he going to attack her?)

(No. He turns quickly and leaves the room.)

(Sobbing, she tries to catch her breath; as she does so –)

*(**BURRAGE** enters.)*

Yes?

BURRAGE. Lunch?

(Blackout.)

ACT THREE

(One year later.)

*(**KELD**'s study again. It's much tidier than before.)*

*(**SHEILA**, lacking a little of her previous sparkle, is entertaining **NAOMI** and **EDMUND**.)*

NAOMI. But you'll come to the meeting, won't you? It will be awfully interesting.

SHEILA. I won't promise, but Keld will go.

EDMUND. That would be wonderful. He's such a great celebrity now, two big dramatic successes in a year, he'd be a splendid acquisition to the club.

SHEILA. He'll be here shortly.

NAOMI. Last night must have been too thrilling; weren't you proud and excited? The papers said the enthusiasm was absolutely boundless.

SHEILA. Oh, first nights are all very much alike.

NAOMI. Yes, but it's different when you happen to *belong* to the author. I shall never forget my feelings when Edmund's first book of poems was published – I was bathed in ecstasy.

EDMUND. I loved you for it, darling.

NAOMI. Was Keld very nervous?

SHEILA. I believe he was; he dined out. I didn't see him until it was nearly over; he came round to my box for a moment during the last act. Are you sure you don't want any more tea, either of you?

NAOMI. Quite, dear, thanks.

(**SHEILA** *rings a bell.*)

EDMUND. Does he do all his work in here?

SHEILA. Yes and he's so sweet about having my tea parties here, it's far cosier than the drawing room.

NAOMI. Where do you write?

SHEILA. Oh, anywhere, in my own room generally, it's nice and quiet.

NAOMI. Yes, quiet is essential, isn't it? I like perfect silence. When is your next book coming out?

SHEILA. I've only done two chapters of it.

NAOMI. You're letting it simmer, I understand. I shall never forget in *The Lips of Love* I came to an impasse. I couldn't write another line, so I just flung it away from me for three months, and when I took it up again the words flowed like...like...

EDMUND. *(Mechanically.)* Molten silver.

(**BURRAGE** *enters and clears away tea things. Exits.*)

(*Then:*)

NAOMI. Yes – molten silver from my pen.

SHEILA. How extraordinary. I'm afraid mine has been left so long that it will be dead when I go back to it, *if* I go back to it.

NAOMI. It's rather wicked of you not to write more, Sheila, people are waiting and watching for your next book. Clara Dewlap was saying only the other day –

SHEILA. I know exactly what Clara Dewlap *would* say, what all my erstwhile literary acquaintances are probably saying, but I can't help it; I don't want to write now, somehow I've got out of the habit of it; after all, there's really no need, Keld is making hundreds.

NAOMI. *(Shocked at such a commercial view.)* But Sheila think of the joy of writing. I sometimes look upon it as a golden key of the cobwebbed gate of the past, a key that one can use at will – to go back and live again those joys and sorrows.

SHEILA. I said all that once, but now I realise I hate the past and everything to do with it.

EDMUND. *(Dreamily.)* The past is but an empty dream

A mist-wrought land of make believe,

In which our mournful memories stray

In search of youthful yesterday!

Who was it said that?

NAOMI. You did dear.

EDMUND. Oh yes, of course, now I remember.

SHEILA. The present *is* happy for me. I shall go to the play again tonight, there have probably been some alterations that I haven't seen yet; besides Keld would like me to go. It's splendid being an author's wife, the management are so awfully nice to me. You know of course, that Keld's historical play is to be produced at the Spinet Theatre next month; that will mean another thrilling first night – you and Edmund really must come with me. I shall have a box of course also a new frock – Keld promised me one.

EDMUND. They described your last night's dress in *The Mirror* this morning.

SHEILA. Did they really? I never saw it. Was my name mentioned?

NAOMI. They said "We noticed the author's wife, Mrs Maxwell, looking very happy and proud of her young husband's success; her dress of blue charmeuse silk edged with silver showed her great charm to full advantage."

SHEILA. Oh, what a pity that I happened to be wearing jet black last night; they're probably mixing me up with Hermione Viking, she was in the next box.

EDMUND. Is Keld just the same as ever, in spite of his success?

SHEILA. Absolutely unspoiled.

EDMUND. How splendid of him!

NAOMI. So few men are clever enough not to be conceited.

(Enter **BURRAGE.***)*

BURRAGE. Miss Raymond has called to the master, ma'am.

SHEILA. Miss Raymond. Oh, well he'll be in very soon; show her up here, Burrage.

BURRAGE. Yes ma'am.

(Exit **BURRAGE.***)*

NAOMI. We really must be going now.

SHEILA. Oh please don't. I'd love you to stay a little longer; you must meet Miss Raymond, she's playing in Keld's first play *The Choice of Evils*.

NAOMI. I know, dear.

EDMUND. Miss Raymond. Is it Ruby Raymond?

SHEILA. Yes.

EDMUND. She used to be at the Gaiety. I remember her quite well.

NAOMI. Really, Edmund? You never mentioned her to me.

*(Re-enter **BURRAGE**.)*

BURRAGE. Miss Raymond.

*(Enter **RUBY RAYMOND** elaborately dressed as usual.)*

*(Exit **BURRAGE**.)*

RUBY. Please forgive me dropping in like this, but I'm longing to hear about the show last night – was it a success?

SHEILA. How nice of you to come. Let me introduce Miss Frith-Bassington and Mr Crowe.

RUBY. Pleased to meet you.

SHEILA. Will you have some tea?

RUBY. No thanks, I've just had some at The Rosebud. They've started *Thé Dansants* there. I went with Irene Harrison, she loves dancing; you'd never think it to look at her. She's playing in *The Choice of Evils* with me, you know, one of my greatest friends.

NAOMI. Do you know I don't think I admire her very much on the stage.

RUBY. Isn't it funny now, most people say that. I think I know what they mean; of course she isn't pretty, and she dresses so badly. Well you must remember she isn't really a clever woman. I've known her a long time now, and she's awfully sweet but no one clever would ever be as jealous as she is over small things. Last week for instance they put my photo in *The Tatler*, quite an original pose up against a screen, and would you believe it, she got a full page in this week! "Miss Harrison in her garden." Well that sort of thing is so small, isn't it? Not that I mind, I mean to say it amuses me, especially since she's never had a garden in her life. Some people have no sense of humour, you know; fancy being taken in a bathing dress with *her* legs.

EDMUND. Why was she wearing a bathing dress in the garden?

RUBY. Oh that was another photo, she's always having them put in; her awful little man does them for her. Everyone laughs when they dance together – but still, I like her. *(Turning to* **SHEILA**.*)* But *do* go on telling me about last night, Mrs Maxwell. Did Keld have to make a speech like he did at our show?

SHEILA. Yes, poor dear, he was horribly nervous.

RUBY. I bet! Was Nellie Grahams there? She said she was going, though how her husband can let her go out looking like she does at the present moment – some women are so brazen; but still I'm frightfully glad it was a success. Aren't you feeling damned proud of Keld? I know I should be if I was his wife.

SHEILA. Of course I am – very proud. Won't you take off your furs?

RUBY. No thanks, I shall be going in a minute, I just dropped in, you know on my way to the Berkeley; I'm dining there with Lord Churchington. I think he's a dear old thing, though everyone runs him down. Of course he gets a bit tight sometimes; but we all have our weaknesses, don't we? He always behaves like a perfect gentleman to me, but then I know how to manage him; if his stories get too hot I just tell him off.

NAOMI. I'm sure that's the only way.

RUBY. When are you coming to the play again Mrs Maxwell? I haven't seen you in front lately.

SHEILA. I've seen it so many times.

RUBY. It's still going wonderfully, but now I suppose you'll be going to the new show all the time; forsaking the old love for the new, I call it. *(She giggles.)*

SHEILA. I don't know that I quite look upon *The Choice of Evils* as an old love. I never thought it a really good play, neither does Keld in his heart of hearts.

RUBY. But it *must* be a good play, it's run nearly a year.

NAOMI. That doesn't always follow, the public are so strange they will sometimes scorn one's most beautiful ideals and simply rave over one's more blatant efforts.

RUBY. *(Quickly.)* I don't think Keld ever makes blatant efforts, do you Mrs Maxwell?

SHEILA. I'm afraid we are all inclined to at times.

RUBY. Oh well, I'll get a blatant effort if I keep Churchie waiting for his dinner – he hates rushing over his food, though he really cares nothing about it. Good-bye, Miss Bassington, pleased to have met you. *(She shakes hands.)* Good-bye. *(She shakes hands with* **EDMUND**.*)*

SHEILA. Won't you stay and see Keld?

RUBY. No, I really haven't the time, but give him my love. Won't you try and persuade him to let me play the lead in his historical play? I'd love to be able to say "Odds bodkins" and "Beshrew me"; it sounds so rude, doesn't it? Good-bye dear.

*(***RUBY** *exits brightly.)*

(Everyone takes a breath.)

NAOMI. Does she often come to see you?

SHEILA. Yes, fairly; Keld is keen on her work, he says she will do great things someday.

NAOMI. *(Cagily.)* I'm sure her Cockney humour is inimitable.

EDMUND. Don't be snobbish Naomi, this is a democratic age.

NAOMI. I'm not in the least snobbish.

SHEILA. I'm afraid I haven't as much faith in Ruby Raymond as Keld has. She's very amusing, as you say Naomi, in her own special line but I don't think she will go much further.

EDMUND. She was very good at the Gaiety.

NAOMI. You seem to have followed her career with great interest Edmund, also with great secrecy; you've never mentioned her to me before.

EDMUND. Now darling, don't be a silly bird. *(To* **SHEILA**.*)* We're so jealous of one another you know, it's too absurd.

NAOMI. I'm certainly not jealous.

EDMUND. My little sweet. *(He kisses her.)* Please excuse me Sheila, you do understand, don't you?

SHEILA. *(Laughing.)* Yes of course.

NAOMI. These men! These men! I know he'll break my heart one day. We really must go now Sheila dear, will you ask Keld about the club for us?

SHEILA. Yes, but are you sure you won't wait for him?

NAOMI. Quite. We shall be terribly late as it is. We have to dine with Psyche Bellamy. Phillip Boblett is going to read one of his plays afterwards; he's an uncouth creature, but I believe very talented.

EDMUND. We've so enjoyed this afternoon.

(Enter **KELD**.*)*

SHEILA. Here is Keld after all.

KELD. Hallo, how are you? *(He shakes hands with both.)*

EDMUND. Splendid thanks.

NAOMI. I'm so glad we just caught you before we went. I want you to become a permanent member of the Next Week Club, instead of just coming occasionally.

KELD. *(Laughing.)* This is very sudden!

NAOMI. But will you? I'll send you a list of the various advantages you will be able to obtain by belonging.

KELD. Are you a member, Sheila?

SHEILA. You know I have been for some time.

KELD. Very well then, if you'll send me the full particulars.

NAOMI. Oh I'm so glad; isn't that splendid, Edmund? Our little mission has been successful. You'll be a tremendous draw, Keld.

KELD. You talk as though it were a kind of music hall.

NAOMI. It really is great fun on Thursday evenings.

KELD. You forget I've spoken there once or twice.

NAOMI. Yes, but only as a guest. By the way, Edmund and I must both congratulate you on your thrilling success last night. Sheila has told us all about it – wonderful! We're coming next week.

KELD. I'm so glad, you must tell me what you think of it.

EDMUND. We will.

NAOMI. We really must go now – it's nearly seven. Come along, Edmund. Good-bye Sheila dear. It *has* been so nice and *do* get on with your book, we're all longing for it. Good-bye Keld.

KELD. Good-bye.

(They all shake hands.)

(Exit **NAOMI** *and* **EDMUND**.*)*

*(***KELD** *falls into a chair.)*

KELD. Have they been here long?

SHEILA. Since about four. You must get them seats for the show.

KELD. I'll leave a note at the box office. How are you darling?

SHEILA. Much the same as usual; nothing out of the way has happened. Today has been rather an anticlimax after last night. I'm tired.

KELD. So am I.

SHEILA. Will you be in for dinner, dear?

KELD. No I'm dining with the Gailbys at the Carlton. I shall have to go and dress soon. Damn it.

SHEILA. Mary Gailby was wearing such a pretty frock the other day; she doesn't look a day over twenty-five.

KELD. She's very attractive. Are there any messages for me?

SHEILA. None. Ruby Raymond came round to hear how the play went. I told her all about it.

KELD. Now wasn't that sweet of her!

SHEILA. Very. I think she wants a part in *The Crusader*. Oh and your new silk hat has come from Barnards, it's up in your room.

KELD. Splendid! By the way what did Naomi say about a book? Have you started a new one?

SHEILA. Good heavens no! She meant *The Shadow Show*. I haven't looked at it for nearly a year.

KELD. Why don't you ever write now, Sheila?

SHEILA. Oh, I don't know. There isn't any need for me to write somehow, you do it all.

KELD. *(Pleased.)* Yes I suppose I do turn out a good hit. Are you happy now Sheila?

SHEILA. Why shouldn't I be?

KELD. I only wondered; you'll tell me if anything goes wrong, any little worries?

SHEILA. Everything is going quite well – it's sweet of you to think of me.

KELD. Not at all – only somehow I should like you to start work again, something to occupy your spare time; it seems such a pity to waste a talent like yours.

SHEILA. For me to write now would necessitate absolute concentration. I don't feel capable of it – there are lots of other things to do.

KELD. Oh Sheila, I wish you were the famous one instead of me; I'd like to be nothing, absolutely nothing. I'm tired tonight; I want to sit at home and rest, and you could read to me and –

SHEILA. Not if I were the famous one. I should be dining at the Carlton with the Gailbys.

KELD. Damn the Gailbys.

SHEILA. You're overreacting, it's only natural after tremendous nerve strain and excitement; why don't you go and lie down.

KELD. Fat lot of time I have to lie down these days.

SHEILA. You can't have everything you know, dear; even success has its trials.

*(Enter **BURRAGE** with piles of evening papers.)*

BURRAGE. They've just sent all these Sir.

KELD. Thank you Burrage.

*(**KELD** takes the papers and commences to look anxiously through them.)*

SHEILA. These will cheer you up, more marvellous notices.

BURRAGE. Can you spare a moment Ma'am?

SHEILA. Yes, what is it?

BURRAGE. Well, the washing has just come home in a shocking state, they seem to get worse and worse at that laundry.

SHEILA. I've written to them twice about it.

BURRAGE. It does seem a shame – that lovely teacloth of yours with iron mould right across it.

SHEILA. Do you think we ought to change again?

BURRAGE. Well Ma'am, if I was you I'd –

KELD. I say, listen to this. *(Reads.)* "Mr Maxwell has certainly excelled himself in *Stress*, produced with enormous success at the Modern Theatre last night. At moments it rises to heights of greatness. Miss Sunderland in particular." – Wait a minute, there's some more about me lower down. Ah! Here it is – "If only all our young playwrights would follow Mr Maxwell's brilliant example and introduce really natural dialogue onto the stage, they would be doing the theatrical profession and the public a signal service!" There, what d'you think of that?

SHEILA. It's wonderful.

KELD. In *The Courier* too; they're generally pretty scathing.

SHEILA. Yes, they are. *(There is silence for a moment.* **KELD** *picks up another paper. Quietly to* **BURRAGE**.*)* But don't you think we ought to give them one more trial? I'll write another note to the manageress. If they send things back badly done again'll go to the Elmtree Laundry; they have motor vans with uniformed drivers. Incidentally they're about three times as expensive, but still –

KELD. Listen, this is rather a nice way of putting it, isn't it? "*Stress* was not only greeted with enthusiasm but genuine enthusiasm, there was none of that forced appreciation one generally sees at first nights nowadays; the debonair author made a witty speech in response to the ecstatic calls for him. He should indeed be proud of a really great achievement. The acting was – well, never mind about *that*.

SHEILA. Splendid. You haven't had one bad review, have you?

KELD. No. *(He continues to look through the papers.)*

BURRAGE. Will that be all Ma'am?

SHEILA. Yes, Burrage.

BURRAGE. Hadn't I better take down the spare room curtains on Monday morning and get Mrs Babin to come in and do them? It seems a pity to trust good lace like that to –

KELD. *(Irritable.)* Oh God!

SHEILA. We'll discuss all that in the morning, Burrage.

BURRAGE. Very good, Ma'am.

(Exit **BURRAGE**.*)*

KELD. Let's talk about the laundry for hours; let's sit round and look at it from all possible points of view; let's compare it with all the other laundries we can think of, let's…

SHEILA. *(Laughing.)* Keld, you are absurd.

KELD. Not at all, I'm serious. I feel that hitherto we have shamefully neglected the laundry; it has not entered into our thoughts enough. Let us conjure up a picture of that lonely laundry, putting iron moulds on your teacloths out of sheer pique – all its feelings outraged by our lack of regard. Why waste our time on idle playwrighting or press notices – let's talk of nothing but the laundry. I say damn the laundry, damn it, damn it, damn it!!

(Exit **KELD** *angrily.* **SHEILA** *sighs.)*

(The front door bell rings. She stops and listens. Then the door bursts open and **OLIVE** *enters.)*

OLIVE. Sheila!

SHEILA. *(Delighted.)* Olive I'd had no idea you were in London, or even England, for that matter – why –

(They embrace.)

OLIVE. I'm up for one night on my way to Scotland; I came straight to you.

SHEILA. Of course you'll stay here?

OLIVE. No thanks, darling, I've booked a room at the St Pancras Hotel – besides, I didn't know for certain you were in town.

SHEILA. I always am.

OLIVE. I haven't seen you for about eight months.

SHEILA. I hate your beastly paper for taking you away so much – but still, as its lucrative, I suppose one mustn't grumble.

OLIVE. It's lucrative of the most wonderful experience as well as money; of course my peculiarly unpleasant nature makes me successful at writing biting revelations about celebrities staying abroad.

SHEILA. I've never read anything of yours that could be called really malicious.

OLIVE. You can't have read many then, dear. I scavenge round foreign hotels in search of juicy scandal like a dog in a dust heap.

SHEILA. It was a bright idea of your editors, but I should imagine pretty expensive.

OLIVE. He gets his money back, the very libelousness of my special page would be enough to sell thousands of copies.

SHEILA. Have there been many lawsuits?

OLIVE. Oh hundreds! But I'm always kept in the background, well out of harm's way. You see, if people knew the identity of the scurrilous scribbler the game would be up.

SHEILA. It sounds a perfectly wonderful job.

OLIVE. I'd give it all up for a quarter of your talent.

SHEILA. *(Holding up her hand.)* Mutual admiration society. Do let's be careful.

OLIVE. It's quite true, I would. This, of course, is interesting and amusing – full of odd adventures – but in reality it's only hack work. There's no art in it, all one needs is a certain amount of observance, absolutely no scruples and a spiteful sense of humour – all of which I possess.

SHEILA. I'm thoroughly envious of you, your life, the wonderful independence of travelling the world, the heaven-sent delight of seeing new places and people, and above all the freedom of it.

OLIVE. *(Laughing.)* Has matrimony brought on the caged-bird feeling already?

SHEILA. *(Listlessly.)* I don't know.

OLIVE. How's Keld?

SHEILA. Very well and doing splendidly – everything he touches now turns to money.

OLIVE. He had a new play produced last night, didn't he? I read something about it in the paper.

SHEILA. Yes, but don't let's talk about it; I've had Edmund and Naomi here all afternoon digging for information. Then Ruby Raymond came –

OLIVE. Of course.

SHEILA. Do you know her?

OLIVE. I know *of* her.

SHEILA. They've all been cross-examining me about the play and what Keld said in his speech, and who was there and what was I wearing! I'm sick to death of the whole thing!

OLIVE. Keld hasn't altered at all – since his success?

SHEILA. He's just the same as he ever was.

OLIVE. You're not though.

SHEILA. What d'you mean?

OLIVE. You're entirely different from when I last saw you.

SHEILA. Different?

OLIVE. You've lost your sparkle, your vitality, you're not nearly as thrilled with things as you were. Don't tell me the worst has happened and we're to expect little clinging fingers and the patter of tiny feet!

SHEILA. *(Half laughing.)* No, it's not as bad as that.

OLIVE. It *is* bad then?

SHEILA. No, it's not *that* bad. I'm merely rather dull, that's all.

OLIVE. What are you working on now?

SHEILA. Nothing.

OLIVE. *(Incredulously.)* So you've actually kept to it.

SHEILA. You mean my vow last year? Yes, I have.

OLIVE. And you feel really happier for it?

SHEILA. Of course I am. Infinitely happier. We never have those rows now; they were so awful, absolutely awful – squabbling and scratchings and making up afterwards. Thank heaven the big row came and cleared the air.

OLIVE. You're going to do no more writing at all?

SHEILA. None. I'm a little dull sometimes, perhaps, but balanced against that is the fact that I have no strain and worry of work – no heated arguments – no moments of black depression when I feel I'm not writing my best – no –

OLIVE. Apparently your life is as carefree as a butterfly's, everything is radiant and beautiful, your husband is successful, you are prosperous, you have found the true happiness – there is nothing left in the world for you to wish for. But all this personal ecstasy has given you tired eyes, Sheila, and a weary droop to your mouth.

SHEILA. You don't understand; there's been a lot of strain during the last week, you see –

OLIVE. I see that there has been a lot more strain the past year.

SHEILA. No Olive, you're wrong, I –

OLIVE. Don't try and deceive me; you're not happy. That's obvious to a blind cat. How could you be happy under the circumstances? Do you think I don't *know*? Other women would be weeping over their husband's faithlessness and screaming for separation or divorce.

SHEILA. *(Slowly.)* What do you mean?

OLIVE. Don't you think we've been pals enough in the past to admit of little more confidence in the present? That sort of thing leaks out – I heard it at Nice. Evangeline Featherstone was there with Billy Grainger; they discussed Keld's mad infatuation quite openly. Of course she said the Raymond woman wasn't worth the –

SHEILA. *(Genuinely shocked.)* Oh – I –

OLIVE. How long have you known?

SHEILA. *(Quietly.)* I didn't – not – not – very long.

OLIVE. It's horrible for you Sheila, and I'm frightfully, frightfully sorry, but heaps of men behave like that; it's considered quite the thing. To shoot a fox or cheat at cards is not cricket, absolutely unforgivable, but to cheat at life as Keld is doing, doesn't matter a bit, they'll take anything and everything you give without a word. In my opinion you've given too much – you've given your brain and your personality. Oh Sheila dear never make another vow like that one.

SHEILA. I did it. I did it for the best.

OLIVE. Poor darling – has it been utterly rotten?

SHEILA. *(Speaking with effort.)* Olive, will you dine with me tonight – out somewhere?

OLIVE. Of course.

SHEILA. You see I feel terribly tired now; I'll take some aspirin and lie down, after that I'll be better able to discuss everything.

OLIVE. *(Rising.)* I understand perfectly. What time shall I call for you?

SHEILA. About half past seven? Will you ring up and get a table? The Ivy, or Petit Savoyard – somewhere quiet.

OLIVE. *(Kissing her.)* Cheer up dear.

SHEILA. *(Trying to smile.)* I'll try.

(Exit **OLIVE***.)*

*(***SHEILA*** stands quite still for a moment and then sits down in a chair facing the audience; she seems dazed.)*

(After a moment **BURRAGE** *enters with a note on a tray.)*

BURRAGE. A note for the master, Ma'am.

SHEILA. Well take it up to him; he's dressing.

BURRAGE. He said he wasn't to be disturbed on any account. I think he's having a short rest.

SHEILA. Leave it here then, Burrage.

BURRAGE. That boy that brought it from the Berkeley said it was *most* important, Ma'am.

SHEILA. *(Starting.)* That'll do Burrage.

BURRAGE. Very good Ma'am.

*(Exit **BURRAGE**.)*

*(**SHEILA** hesitates for a moment, then she takes the note and turns it over in her hands, then quite calmly she opens it and reads it. When she has finished she crumples it in her hand and closes her eyes for a moment as though the effort of realising everything is too much for her.)*

*(Then she clenches her hands with a sort of concentrated quiet fury, she picks up the poker and going to **KELD**'s desk, she breaks it open – sparing no noise in the process. This done, she searches through all the drawers and pigeon holes, scattering papers everywhere.)*

(At last she discovers a pack of letters; she compares the writing with the crumpled letter in her hand.)

*(Enter **KELD** in a dressing gown.)*

KELD. What are you doing?

SHEILA. *(Quietly.)* Don't bluster. It's no use. I've found out everything.

KELD. Look here Sheila, you don't understand.

SHEILA. I do understand Keld.

KELD. Give me those letters.

SHEILA. Certainly.

> *(She throws them at his feet. He picks them up and makes a move to go.)*

Don't go, I want to speak to you.

KELD. You've made the biggest mistake in your life. How dare you break open my desk? Do you think that sort of trick ever does any good?

SHEILA. I don't care.

KELD. You're being unnecessarily dramatic.

SHEILA. We have to face facts, beastly, incredible facts: this situation we've so often refused to write about because it was too hackneyed. Now we're living it and we can't get away.

KELD. If only you'd let me explain.

SHEILA. I thought at least that you were above making excuses.

KELD. Sheila try to understand. You think because I chose to flirt with Ruby that –

SHEILA. Flirt? With Ruby? If that were the end of it, but – spare me Keld. I wonder if you'll ever realise what you've done. You've killed my heart stone cold dead. I'm numb – you've taken everything from me; I allowed you to because I hoped it might ultimately lead to happiness, but it hasn't; it has only led to deception and lying and making love to a –

> *(She stops.)*

I don't love you anymore now. I hate you. I hate you. I've put up with your intolerances, your selfishness, all because I felt that you loved *me* in spite of everything, and that it would all come right in the end and somehow we'd live happily ever after. I haven't written a word because we couldn't both write – that was proved a year ago. I gave up my working brain for you. I've devoted all my time to household affairs; I've let myself be worried over washing bills and new servants. The miserable drudgery of the mind. That is how I've given up my intellect for you, and through it all I've loved you, unfalteringly, and that is how I've given up my intelligence for you.

KELD. Sheila, let me explain.

SHEILA. Do you think it's necessary?

KELD. Yes, I do. I'm going to make excuses for myself as well – why shouldn't I? You've been different during the last year and you know it. You left. You only pretended to take the slightest interest in my plays. I've been working terribly hard lately and naturally I needed diversion. I looked to you, but you weren't ready to help, you didn't realise it – so I went to Ruby Raymond. I don't love her, I swear, I don't. I never could but she's there when I want her, amusing and frivolous, an absolute contrast to any woman I've ever met. I've been a cad – I know now – forgive me for my beastly tempers, forgive me for my selfishness in every way, and above all forgive me for being untrue to you. You say you've loved me all this time – give me one more chance – I'd do anything to win you back to me. All this year, I honestly didn't know you hated it so, you seemed so content, so happy –

SHEILA. *(Losing control.)* Content! Happy! I loathed every minute of it; I was sick with the nauseating drudgery, and you say I seemed content. Couldn't you see, couldn't you see even that? You make your stupid weak excuses, your need for diversion and change – and I wasn't ready to help you because I didn't realise what you needed? The last's true, I didn't, I could never realise your despicable behaviour until it was banged into my brain by proof, hard bitter proof. I'm finished with you, utterly, entirely finished. I don't want a penny of your money. I don't want to hear of you or see you again, ever in my entire life. I mean it – from the bottom of my heart. I'm done with you – done with you!

> *(She goes out of the room, slamming the door behind her.* **KELD** *slowly tears the letters into pieces and throws them into the fire. He falls into a chair stunned and weeping.)*
>
> *(Curtain.)*

ACT FOUR

(Four months later.)

(The living room of a cottage in Cornwall.)

(It is late afternoon.)

*(**OLIVE** is tidying her hair.)*

*(**KELD** is looking anxiously out the window.)*

OLIVE. Doesn't one look perfectly awful after a railway journey, a kind of greeny colour.

*(**KELD** says nothing. He goes on looking out of the window.)*

Thank you Keld, you are a great comfort.

KELD. What can have happened to her?

OLIVE. She didn't expect us until tomorrow.

KELD. She didn't expect "us" at all, she only expected you.

OLIVE. If Sheila is anything like the psychologist she pretends to be she'd guess that I, with my soft appealing nature, would at least make some sort of an effort to reunite you two yearning souls.

KELD. I wish you wouldn't be so flippant.

OLIVE. My dear Keld, I took you seriously all the way from Exeter to Plymouth – when we were passing such nice scenery, too – you can't expect me to keep on with it.

KELD. You're behaving like this because you're really just as miserably nervous as I am.

OLIVE. You're right but it does no good to admit it. I wish Burrage would hurry up with the tea, that'll buck us both up.

KELD. She won't understand, I know she won't. Why should she take me back? Four months is a long time, even if she missed me a bit at first, that's all over now –

OLIVE. Don't talk about being "taken back" in that abased manner, as a matter of fact she was nearly much to blame as you in the first place – making stupid vows and being idiotic enough to stick to them. Only one thing really matters, and that is whether she is still in love with you; if she is all will be well.

KELD. *(Seriously.)* Olive, I wish I were you – sitting back smiling and looking on, giving a useful bit of advice here and a damnable little bit of common sense there. You're glad when things go right and sorry when they go wrong – in moderation; but at heart you're so unmoved by all this, while I'm feeling so desperate and hopeless, you're just wanting your tea and hoping for the best.

OLIVE. Considering that I've dragged you down here, like a benevolent fairy godmother in order to try and put everything right *and* gone to endless trouble for you both, it's hardly nice of you to lash me with your tongue.

KELD. I wasn't. I really wasn't. You've been perfectly wonderful. Whatever happens, you've been more helpful than any fairy godmother, however benevolent. I was only just envying you.

*(Enter **BURRAGE** with tea and toast.)*

BURRAGE. I've toasted the splits for you Ma'am.

OLIVE. Thank you so much Burrage. I suppose you haven't any idea how far Mrs Maxwell was going this afternoon?

BURRAGE. She said something about Kynance Cove, it's a long way, across the moors, but she generally gets back about this time.

KELD. It wouldn't be any use going out to meet her?

OLIVE. No I shouldn't think it would. Thank you Burrage.

(Exit BURRAGE.)

Sit down Keld dear, worrying won't do any good. You were right when you said I was as nervous as you are, and quite wrong when you accused me of being unmoved and smiling. I'm not smiling. I'm hating it – but there's one comfort and that is that you're doing the right thing, keep that in your mind. Now have some tea.

(She pours it out.)

KELD. What shall I do if she refuses to listen to me?

OLIVE. She won't refuse to listen.

KELD. *(Taking tea.)* Assuming she does and comes back to me, do you think things will go on running smoothly? I mean after the first flush of happiness has died away. Is it hopeless for us to try and live together?

OLIVE. Not at all. Now you've both had quite a lot of unhappiness and hopefully learnt a bit.

KELD. I don't want her not to write anymore; she *must* go on with it, whatever happens. Will you tell her that?

OLIVE. You'll be able to tell her yourself.

KELD. No, no *you* tell her – you see her first, oh please, please do. I'll wait outside on the cliff and you can signal to me if it's all right.

OLIVE. Coward.

KELD. *(Passionately.)* It isn't cowardice at all. It's sense. If she suddenly sees me here it will be a great shock. She'll probably be furious at being taken unawares. I *know* Sheila. If you talked to her first, found out how she really felt towards me –

OLIVE. I was rather relying on that shock.

KELD. Please Olive, do what I ask. I don't think I can bear to take the risk of surprising her. I'm so worried and anxious I'll probably be foolish and tactless from sheer nerves. It means everything in the world to me. I never realised how much I wanted her until I came into this room – it's full of her things – books and photographs – all the absurd sentiment we'd always laugh at – we may quarrel and bicker 'til doomsday but she must come back! She must, she must, she must!

OLIVE. What can I say to her? In all probability she'll be terribly angry with me.

KELD. Olive, please – please don't fail me now, you've been so sympathetic and so splendid all along, help me at the last lap, make an effort –

OLIVE. You can't go and wait out on the cliff. It's raining quite hard.

KELD. I don't care. I'll tell you something Olive. I've existed without her for four months, thinking that if I stood it long enough time would dull the misery of it; then you came and put me firmly in the wrong, which was where I should've put myself from the very beginning. Since then the longing for her has been ten thousand times worse. I daren't allow myself to think of us being together again, in case it all falls through, in case I fail to convince her that I love her, and now – it all depends on what transpires during the next hour. Olive, I feel as if I were going mad.

OLIVE. It's all right Keld, I understand. I'll do what I can, you'd better go out now at once.

KELD. You'll call me – if – when –

OLIVE. Yes! Now then go quickly, here's your hat.

KELD. *(At door.)* I'll be over there, just behind that shed! I'll be able to see her come in.

OLIVE. Go!

>*(**OLIVE** shuts the door after him.)*

>*(Enter **BURRAGE**.)*

BURRAGE. Oh I heard the door go, I thought it was the mistress.

OLIVE. No Burrage, it was only Mr Maxwell going out. I think he's walking a little way in the hopes of finding her.

BURRAGE. He'll get wet.

OLIVE. He won't mind that.

BURRAGE. He might have taken that Mackintosh.

OLIVE. Tell me Burrage, has your mistress been well during these last few weeks?

BURRAGE. Yes Ma'am, working hard and taking a lot of exercise.

OLIVE. Working?

BURRAGE. Her writing. She's taken it up again with a vengeance, at it all day she is.

OLIVE. I'm glad of that.

BURRAGE. So am I, Ma'am.

OLIVE. And she's quite happy and comfortable?

BURRAGE. No one could be comfortable in a place with no electric light or gas, no hot water laid on, miles from anywhere, and a kitchen that covers you in soot if you even look at it, *but* she's certainly happier than I've seen her in years.

(**BURRAGE** *smiles.*)

OLIVE. *Really?*

BURRAGE. She's free again, that's what it is, it only bears out what I've always said – marriage is a trap.

OLIVE. You've never been married, have you Burrage?

BURRAGE. No Ma'am, not *married*.

OLIVE. Then how can you tell if it's a trap or not?

BURRAGE. By the way other people behave. You see the trouble is no woman can ever really know what a man's like until she's lived with him for a time, then it's too late to do anything about it. Being with them all the time I watched the master and the mistress carefully, you couldn't help noticing things. She used to feel she ought to give into him over trifles and he used to take it all for granted, any man would, it's human nature. They used to have awful arguments over things, and she used to win but pretend he had for the sake of peace. I always knew trouble was bound to come. The one thing love never teaches you is how to manage each other.

OLIVE. I never realised Burrage that you were a creature of such experience.

BURRAGE. I've seen a lot one way or another; I've had my moments.

OLIVE. And you think it turned out for the best?

BURRAGE. I do Ma'am, I do. She's independent now and working with nothing to worry about.

OLIVE. Nothing to worry about?

BURRAGE. No Ma'am, I don't think she'll make the same mistake again in a hurry.

OLIVE. How do you mean?

BURRAGE. I think I'm rather sorry for the master now, though he brought it on himself.

(*Exit* **BURRAGE**.)

(**OLIVE** *is alone for a moment pondering what* **BURRAGE** *has said.*)

(*Enter* **SHEILA** *in a wet coat. She is surprised to see* **OLIVE**.)

SHEILA. Olive my dear! This is wonderful. Why didn't you let me know you were coming a day earlier?

OLIVE. I thought I'd surprise you.

SHEILA. You have! Beautifully! (*She removes her coat.*) You've had some tea?

OLIVE. Oh yes, it saved my life after that beastly train.

SHEILA. If you'd have wired, I'd have met you at Helston.

OLIVE. No human could've borne that bus ride both ways, it nearly jerked my inside out.

SHEILA. Locomotion is still primitive here. Pour me some tea, would you? I'm rather damp.

OLIVE. Sit down and tell me everything, I haven't seen you in so long.

(**OLIVE** *hands* **SHEILA** *a cup of tea.*)

SHEILA. You probably have much more news than I have.

OLIVE. No, I want to hear about you. Burrage says you're writing again.

SHEILA. Yes I am. I've finished *The Shadow Show*.

OLIVE. *The Shadow Show?*

SHEILA. Yes, the novel I started when I was first married and then *(She pauses.)* let it simmer for nearly a year.

OLIVE. Yes. I remember. Are you pleased with it now?

SHEILA. *(Quietly.)* It's quite the best thing I've done, but more to the point Claverton and Lake are pleased too. They've written ecstatic letters simply raving and they're bringing it out extra early.

OLIVE. Sheila! How splendid.

SHEILA. *(Without the slightest bit of enthusiasm.)* Yes, isn't it?

OLIVE. You don't appear particularly thrilled about it.

SHEILA. I'm not.

OLIVE. Are you happy?

SHEILA. What a silly question. It's so difficult to be happy.

OLIVE. *(Abruptly.)* Sheila, I have something to confess. I brought Keld down with me today. He's out there on the cliff now – waiting.

SHEILA. I know.

OLIVE. You know?

SHEILA. Yes I know, I saw him as I came by. He didn't see me though. Why did you do it?

OLIVE. Because he's so utterly wretched without you and has been all along. He's aching for you to go back to him. You *must* go back to him.

SHEILA. I'm going back to him all right – you'd better call him in, he'll catch cold out there in the rain.

OLIVE. Sheila, I'm so glad.

SHEILA. Don't be, Olive.

OLIVE. Sheila?

SHEILA. Call him in.

OLIVE. But Sheila –

SHEILA. *(Quietly.)* I've been down here for four months now Olive. Alone except for Burrage. I've sat in this room on grey leaden days and watched the rain trickling down the windows; feeling as though the weight of everything were driving me mad. I've tramped across the moors in the shrieking winds and wandered like a lost soul through the Scotch mists all the time getting things straightened out in my mind and now I've succeeded. I can see ahead clearly and dispassionately. I thought intellect counted in married life when things went wrong – but it didn't – we behaved exactly like everyone else at the crucial moment.

OLIVE. Sheila?

SHEILA. You can call Keld in. I'm ready to talk things over.

*(**OLIVE** goes to the door and calls to **KELD**.)*

*(She turns to **SHEILA**.)*

OLIVE. I've been away from you so long that I've lost the trick of reading your thoughts like I used to.

SHEILA. Dear Olive.

I'm afraid you're about to be disappointed. It won't be a rapturous, sentimental reconciliation with tears of joy coursing down everybody's cheeks; it will probably be rather dull from a dramatic point of view. You see, I don't love him anymore.

*(Enter **KELD**.)*

KELD. Sheila!

SHEILA. Come in and get warm.

KELD. *(Looking at **OLIVE**.)* Is it all right?

OLIVE. I don't know.

KELD. Sheila, have you forgiven me?

SHEILA. Yes.

KELD. Will you come back to me?

SHEILA. *With* you, yes.

KELD. *(Not noticing the difference.)* May I kiss you again?

SHEILA. Keld. (**OLIVE** *starts to leave the room.*) No Olive, don't go.

OLIVE. I think I'd rather –

SHEILA. *(Quietly and emphatically.)* I want you to be here. Come and sit down. Keld you sit down as well. There are lots of things to say.

KELD. Sheila give me your hand. I'm wretchedly humble.

SHEILA. Don't be humble, that's all over.

KELD. I want you to come back and make a fresh start. I want your help –

SHEILA. I want your help as well. But let's not deceive ourselves. How can we make a fresh start with all our illusions and dreams broken up behind us? We've just got to go on and make the best of the situation.

KELD. You're being so cold. Do you love me at all anymore?

SHEILA. No.

OLIVE. Sheila, don't be so cruel.

SHEILA. I'm not cruel. I can't help not loving him.

KELD. I don't understand.

OLIVE. Why are you going back to him then? If you don't love him, if you're not happy, if you're writing again. What's the point?

SHEILA. Oh Olive, Olive – don't you see?

OLIVE. *(Looking at her.)* See? See what? – Oh.

KELD. What? Olive what? Sheila what?

SHEILA. I'm going to have a child.

KELD. *(Incredulous.)* Sheila!

SHEILA. Don't look at me like that.

KELD. When did you know?

SHEILA. The first week I came down here.

KELD. Oh Sheila darling –

SHEILA. You're glad?

KELD. Yes, I am. *(Pause.)* Terribly glad. Yes.

SHEILA. Well it *frightens* me.

OLIVE. The first week and you never let me know?

SHEILA. You were in Sweden working hard and besides, it was better for me to face things myself.

KELD. Sheila, I love you so. This is another chance for us both.

SHEILA. No it's another chance for you. I don't need another chance.

KELD. I'll do anything in the world to make you happy. Love me again – please, please, please love me again.

SHEILA. For now Keld, we will be together. But I don't love you, in fact I've found I can thrive without you. But these circumstances dictate something else. Something that I don't wish to challenge. And God forgive me but I need you now.

KELD. Darling!

SHEILA. I loved you passionately once, I might regain that love. For now though I can't, I simply can't.

KELD. I will change.

SHEILA. Perhaps.

OLIVE. So…?

SHEILA. It's done. In name only.

> (**KELD** *carefully considers his response, then…*)

KELD. As you wish.

> (**SHEILA** *reaches for* **OLIVE***'s hand.*)

SHEILA. I feel so alone and dreadfully frightened.

> (**OLIVE** *holds* **SHEILA** *while* **KELD** *looks on helplessly as the curtain falls.*)

The End

www.ingramcontent.com/pod-product-compliance
Ingram Content Group UK Ltd.
Pitfield, Milton Keynes, MK11 3LW, UK
UKHW021847220126
467242UK00004B/21